SURVIVAL OF DEATH

SURVIVAL OF DEATH

by
PAUL BEARD

"Which, like the toad, ugly and venomous,
Wears yet a precious jewel in his head."
As You Like It
Act 2, Scene I

PILGRIM BOOKS
TASBURGH NORWICH ENGLAND

Copyright © 1966 by Paul Beard

First published 1966
Second impression 1972, third impression 1983
This impression 1988

ISBN 0 946259 25.9

Printed in Great Britain
at the University Printing House, Oxford
by David Stanford
Printer to the University

FOR PATIENT

ROSE

WITH LOVE

Foreword

BY THE REV. LESLIE D. WEATHERHEAD,

C.B.E., M.A., PH.D., D.D., D.LITT.

I HAVE long prophesied that the area of enquiry vaguely indicated by the words "Psychic Research" will yield most enriching discoveries if it is explored by those who bring to it the kind of mental discipline and ability to examine evidence which is shown by scientists in material fields like biology, physics, chemistry and astronomy.

I commend this book enthusiastically because it is quite outstanding as a discussion of the evidence for and against the human survival of death.

The Christian Church has offered affirmation and consolation. Spiritualism has offered alleged communications. Mr. Beard offers evidence with a quality of analytical detachment, which, to my mind, is exactly what is so badly needed. In the end he regards the evidence as sufficiently conclusive to warrant belief in survival, but he examines every possible alternative interpretation of the phenomena and is never woolly, or afraid of where his investigations may lead. He concedes every possible claim that telepathy and clairvoyance may account for many alleged "messages from the dead", but he finds a residue in the evidence for which the most intelligent and reasonable explanation is that of survival.

No reader can fail to be convinced of the author's complete integrity and fairness, or of his ability and insight. Those who feel that there must be something in "spiritualism" but who are cut off by manifestations from Red Indian chiefs, by baby voices and broken English, by mediums on this side of death and controls on the other, by trivial messages and exaggerated claims, should read this book.

In it all the relevant phenomena are examined unemotionally, chaff is separated from grain, and a reflection on the evidence is offered in exactly the mental temper so badly needed in a world which is tired of materialism and its rejection of any alleged reality outside its scope.

I welcome the book with all my heart and hope it will have the wide circulation which it deserves.

Acknowledgments

MY THANKS are due to the Society for Psychical Research and the Editor of *Proceedings* for permission to publish many extracts therefrom; I would like to make it clear that the Society holds no corporate views, and the opinions expressed in its publications are those of the authors alone.

I should also like to thank Miss Geraldine Cummins for her generous permission to quote freely from *The Road to Immortality* and the present publishers, the Psychic Press; and from *Swan on a Black Sea*, and the publishers, Messrs. Routledge & Kegan Paul Ltd., to whom thanks are also due for an extract from *On the Threshold of the Unseen* by Sir W. Barrett; Messrs. G. Bell & Sons Ltd. for quotations from *Evidence of Identity* by Kenneth Richmond and *Evidence of Personal Survival from Cross-Correspondences* by H. F. Saltmarsh; Messrs. Collins and the Exor. of the Rev. C. Drayton Thomas for extracts from *Life Beyond Death with Evidence*; Messrs. Chatto and Windus Ltd. for a passage from *The Sixth Sense* by Rosalind Heywood and to Messrs. E. P. Dutton & Co. Inc. in respect of the American edition, published under the title of *Beyond the Reach of Sense*; Messrs. Hamish Hamilton Ltd. for a quotation from *The Millionth Chance* by James Leasor; Messrs. Hodder and Stoughton Ltd. for extracts from *The Light and the Gate* by Prof. Raynor C. Johnson; Messrs. Longmans, Green & Co. Ltd. for passages from *Personality Survives Death* by Lady Florence E. Barrett; Penguin Books Ltd. for a quotation from Prof. C. A. Mace's Foreword to *Experimental Psychical Research* by Doctor Robert H. Thouless, and the same publishers and Messrs. Hughes Massie Ltd. for a quotation from *The Personality of Man* by G. N. M. Tyrrell; the Editor of *The Quarterly Review of The Churches' Fellowship for Psychical and Spiritual Studies* for extracts from articles on the R.101 Disaster; Charles C. Thomas, Publisher, Springfield, Illinois, U.S.A. and Messrs. Rider & Co. Ltd. and the Hutchinson Publishing Group and Messrs. Laurence Pollinger Ltd. for a quotation from *The Enigma of Survival* by Prof. Hornell Hart, and the same publishers for two extracts from *When We Wake* by M. H. Collyer and E. P. Dampier; the Spiritualist Press for extracts from *No Living Person Could Have Known* by W. F. Neech; the Editor of *Two Worlds* for a quotation from Silver Birch; Messrs. John M. Watkins and the author for a quotation from *Private Dowding*, and for quotations from *Discarnate Influence in Human Life* by Prof. Ernesto Bozzano; the White Eagle Publishing Trust for extracts from the White Eagle Student Teachings and from *The Return of Arthur Conan Doyle* by Ivan Cooke. I also acknowledge with thanks the use of brief extracts from *Thirty Years of Psychical Research* by Prof. Charles Richet (Messrs. Collins) and from *Tea with Walter de la Mare* by Russell Brain (Messrs. Faber & Faber Ltd.). If I have unwittingly overlooked any source from which permission should have been sought, or have failed to trace it, I must ask for indulgence accordingly.

I would cordially thank the member of the S.P.R. who has allowed me to quote from a private experience.

Finally I would like to record my appreciation of long-suffering personal friends who have gone to great trouble in criticising my manuscript and making valuable suggestions for its improvement.

Contents

FOREWORD BY THE REV. LESLIE D. WEATHERHEAD,
C.B.E., M.A., PH.D., D.D., D.LITT. vii

PART ONE: THE PROBLEM

| Chapter One | TWO WITNESSES | 3 |

PART TWO: RESEARCH

Chapter Two	EVIDENCE FROM PSYCHICAL RESEARCH	13
Chapter Three	HYPOTHESES POINTING AWAY FROM SURVIVAL	29
Chapter Four	FURTHER DIFFICULTIES	48
Chapter Five	TEST CASES	53
Chapter Six	SUBJECTIVE FACTORS IN RESEARCH	64

PART THREE: SEARCH

Chapter Seven	DIFFICULTIES IN PERSONAL EVIDENCE	75
Chapter Eight	DIFFICULTIES OF COMMUNICATION	89
Chapter Nine	THE MEDIUM	101
Chapter Ten	THE TRANCE PERSONALITY	112
Chapter Eleven	SEARCH AND RESEARCH	131
Chapter Twelve	SUMMING-UP	153

BOOKS FOR FURTHER READING 171
INDEX 175

PART ONE
The Problem

CHAPTER ONE

Two Witnesses

I

SHALL I survive death? Nobody fails, of course, at some period of life to ask that question, but to ask and to answer are, alas, two very different things indeed. Some prefer never to answer, to say that nobody knows or can know. Then perhaps one day life poses the question in a wholly new and very disturbing form – has someone who has recently died, who was dearly loved, truly passed into nothingness? If not, can he or she prove it by unmistakably speaking once again to the bereft? The questioner may begin, for the first time, to investigate for himself.

He will find that to obtain evidence concerning survival of death is at once extremely easy and extraordinarily difficult: that the evidence has in fact produced two quite different answers. The first answer, based on psychical research, carried out in an objective and scientific spirit, can be said to be that survival is not so far a necessary hypothesis to account for the available evidence; that during unusual states of consciousness information is given which purports to come from the minds of dead men and women, but that it is not impossible, and in some cases likely or even certain, that it is derived from the minds of the living; that although there is some of this evidence which is hard to explain, except in extremely intricate ways, by any other hypothesis than that of survival, nevertheless further investigation may eventually find a normal explanation for all the evidence. To those who wish to enter upon an objective study, the Society for Psychical Research, without holding any corporate views, offers its own fifty-odd substantial volumes of *Proceedings*, and many other volumes have been published, in England and elsewhere, similarly based on scientific observations.

The second, and different answer, is primarily based upon private and personal experiences. Many people, some of whom have a vested religious interest in the matter, others not, have come to accept, as a result of their investigations, that abundant, and at times convincing, evidence of survival has reached them, and that other people, if they wish, are likely to be able to obtain similar direct personal evidence for themselves. Their viewpoint also is supported by many volumes of evidence. Their methods are not scientific methods, although in some cases they are orderly methods; the problem is to assess whether or not they have a validity of their own, of a different kind to that of psychical research, and which the present findings of the latter need not necessarily set aside. Is psychical research the only proper canon? If not, by what canons can direct personal experience properly be judged?

Why are these two answers so different? Why, in so momentous an issue, do these two sets of evidence, these two approaches, contradict each other so greatly, or seem to? Can it be that each is really looking at a different set of facts within the same material? Are the differences as real as they seem? Can they partly be reconciled in any way? If so, how far does each set overlap the other? Is there not something in common which they can agree upon? How can the real value in each be eventually determined? Is one so much more valuable as to make the other unnecessary, or does each have an inalienable veracity of its own? Where does the truth rest?

2

Formal scientific interest can be said to have begun in 1882, when the Society for Psychical Research was set up, led by a small group of Cambridge philosophers and scientists; its object was not primarily directed towards the problem of survival, but towards the study of seemingly unusual human powers, telepathic powers, what is now usually called extra-sensory perception, or ESP, for some of the scientific members of the Society had a private prior expectation that orderly investigation would probably soon sweep away all that passed for evidence of survival. They expected that some of this apparent evidence would be shown as capable of ordinary rational explanation, and most or all of the rest shown up as superstition or plain fraud. Yet, as the work of the Society proceeded upon its orderly, scientific way, this did not happen. The evidence could never wholly be disposed of, nor, on the other hand, though much of it came to point towards survival, has it been accepted as conclusive. From the evidence in the S.P.R. records, or obtained elsewhere by similarly scientific methods, as the years have gone by, some scientists have accepted survival as a working hypothesis, and some have in addition reached personal conviction of survival; others think that the evidence is not strong enough to set up any hypothesis. After examining the same evidence, scientists of equal standing have thus found themselves led into opposite directions. At first sight, it would seem an obvious conclusion that it is best that it shall be left to science to go on working patiently in its own way until sooner or later it settles the matter decisively to the satisfaction of all.

But the matter is far less simple than this. For the evidence, even that part of it directly observed scientifically, is necessarily permeated at times by other factors which cannot be scientifically measured. The scientific part is hard to hive off from these other factors.

Psychical research aims, of course, at being completely objective; its mesh does not trap subjective judgments. It cannot *measure*, for instance, a person's memory of a dead friend, nor how it corresponds with the total image of this person presented through a medium. It can count the facts and say how many are stated accurately or inaccurately, can record, to take a brief illustration from the *Proceedings of the S.P.R.*, that the alleged communicator, as presented through the medium's trance, manages with difficulty to make the medium's lips say "Orfen" instead of "Of-ten" as the medium normally pronounces it, and that in the person of the entranced medium she inclines her head in a characteristic way continually to the right, both of which she did whilst alive on earth. It can record that she gives correctly the meaning of "poon", a private word used during her life between her and the investigators, and eventually after considerable difficulty produces its companion word "sporkish".* But there is much in what makes up the whole characteristic picture of this soi-disant communicating personality, which cannot be represented by counting facts, and which rests upon the sitter's subjective estimate of it. Such material is found both inside and outside psychical research. When the psychical researcher encounters personal evidence of his own, he has to give judgment on it not only as a scientist, but also from a different standpoint as a private person, that person within him who looks out from over the shoulder of his other, scientific self. He looks at some parts of

* *Proceedings of the S.P.R.*, Vol. 30, pp. 445, 481.

it scientifically, and other parts privately. He is dealing with two different sorts of facts.

As a scientist he can only be interested in that part of the evidence which can be equally well assessed by a third party who was never present at that seance, and who has never met either the living or the dead persons involved. The personally assessable parts of the testimony cannot be made scientific fact.

Scientific discipline pays very strict attention to the necessary limitations which its own methods impose upon it, and whilst it cannot eliminate from psychical research those subjective aspects of its evidence which bear directly upon survival, it has to confine itself to judging their factual content. These subjective and factual contents are sometimes so closely interwoven that they are hard to separate out completely from one another.

Now the subjective aspects which psychical research discards because they are not capable of forming part of scientific evidence may be significant by other standards; may fall within other modes of observation with disciplines of their own. These are the factors that independent investigators, as well as those who can be called survivalists, take account of and to which they bring their own independent honesty of judgment.

Through the mesh of the scientific net, or outside it altogether, swim these other fish which science cannot catch. To describe the sort of fish which escape this scientific net is not altogether easy. It is not a matter of different and lower standards in the sense that proof in the law-court falls far short of the standards of scientific proof. It arises from a different quality of attention on the part of the observer.

3

Science stands apart from the vested interests involved in human emotions. It stands wholly aside from the urgent need to *know for oneself* whether one survives. Not all men are content to leave the problem of survival for science to settle at some indefinite future date; they ask if there are other, swifter ways to the truth. They take heart from the fact that if science does finally show it to be true, does finally give its seal of approval, survival will already have been true meanwhile, when it still remained under scientific doubt. However, such views, if they are to be held, ignore scientific opinion at their peril, for of course they can be the product of mere foolishness, or of a credulity which is unfortunate, vain or sad.

Danger or no danger, the search for the meanings of life and death has to go on being explored through many other temperaments besides that of the man of science. It is not disputed that a poem can never be evaluated in scientific terms, not at least the poetry in it; nor can a historical event or a mystical experience. These have to be understood and judged by other human faculties. Similarly, non-scientific faculties can also be brought to explore the varying facets of evidence of survival.

For investigation can be more than an enquiry, it can also become an experience. A man's own experience of communication can be real in a different way from that in which scientific proof is regarded as real. However varying its value, each man can make, through his private experience, his own special contribution to the general pool. However, private experience, unfortunately, is partly incommunicable. What gives it strength to the recipient – the part of the experience which is uniquely his own – is the very thing which gives it weakness as evidence. Such testimony indeed has its shortcomings, but then so have scientific records, which, however complete within themselves, are necessarily confined to their own differently selective set of observations.

4

This book will not deal with any of the physical happenings investigated by psychical research. It is not concerned with such evidence as is available of the seance-room phenomena of apparent movement of objects at a distance from the medium; nor with levitations, with poltergeist disturbances, with the transport of objects from a distance, nor with "materialisations" which are said to speak, and to inhale and exhale; nor with raps and tambourines; nor spirit photographs or writing between slates; it does not deal with substantial loss of weight in a medium during her seance and the return to her normal weight afterwards; nor with the appearance of hands which, when investigators required it of them, allowed wax casts to be made from which the hands then withdrew without breaking the cast. It does not discuss the production of voices through a trumpet in English and in foreign languages.

The reason for not referring to these is two-fold. This sort of evidence is based on sense-observation; some of it has been observed by well-qualified scientists; but because it is not repeatable at will, the correctness of the observations has been criticised, especially after the scientists who made them have died.

Evidence of such kind weakens with time, especially if besides being unrepeatable at the scientist's will it is not in fact repeated (a quite different thing), or only very seldom repeated. Psychical research has also amply demonstrated by experiment how fallible human observation is, even when it is trained. Future evidence will doubtless be dealt with by apparatus for measurement which had not been developed when most of these phenomena took place, but up to the present physical phenomena have almost always been subsequently questioned and doubted; they are a particularly happy hunting ground for later sceptics who do not suffer from the handicap of having been actually present at the time.

That is the first reason for ignoring purported physical happenings. The second lies in the belief that the future is unlikely to belong to any such physical phenomena, which, considered as a mode of communication, have at best been crude and limited. Fundamentally they seem incapable of much development in this direction.

The future is much more likely to lie in the mental field, because here the evidence does not depend upon fallible observation, but is based upon written communications or on spoken ones which have been recorded verbatim. Although the real source of this evidence can be extremely hard to establish, its *existence*, unlike that of physical phenomena, is unchallengeable. This mental field can be and has been examined by scientific methods. It can also be the subject of direct personal experience. It has the advantage that it is capable of being examined by both methods. In this field much work remains to be done, both to obtain further evidence and to try and discover if and how far it is possible to improve the quality, reliability and precision of alleged communications.

Many men and women of integrity and intelligence with time and patience can make contributions of direct value in the personal sector of this fascinating field. Before making the first practical approach, however, an intending worker will find it worth asking what –

assuming that it were possible for it to be provided – he would accept as valid evidence of survival. Having done this – and it is indeed no easy task – a further question then needs to be asked immediately. If this evidence were to come to him, would he then find that he would after all feel it necessary to change his ground, and decide he must ask for some further evidence still? And if he were given this further evidence, would he provide still further demands to be met? If so, is it because he is already committed to a view of life in which survival is deemed impossible, and his enquiry is therefore, however subtly, being prejudged? Or is this hesitation only due to a proper caution, or to the strangeness of the notion of there being any possible reality in such an approach? Does it point to a coming battle between the evidence and his present philosophy?

There are many reasons for reluctance towards the seeming evidence for survival. The facts, *if* there be facts, will have to bear a heavier burden before they can become established than is borne by very many scientifically observed facts which have no important moral or philosophical implications. There must be a process of interaction with the mind and feelings of the enquirer, which at the start may regard the facts, or apparent facts, as alien or impossible. The enquirer may find himself embarked on a long and unexpected journey.

It is a complex field of study where scientific investigations, personal philosophies, and religious concepts meet and overlap. If the evidence comes to improve in quality over the years, it may gradually bring these shifting fields into some sort of closer alignment. It might one day even become a fruitful meeting ground. So far there has been found embedded in the evidence for survival a number of baffling, worthless and disconcerting features which have helped to make it a kind of disreputable poor relation of all, of science, religion and personal philosophy alike, disowned more often than acknowledged.

On the other hand it does also present a number of startling and vivid facts, which, for many people, have pointed significantly towards survival. Difficulties of many kinds lie unresolved in this apparently contradictory field. No easy task lies before any new investigator who, from whatever point of view, decides to approach the challenge, alike fascinating and baffling, which awaits whatever skills he is able to bring to its study.

PART TWO

Research

CHAPTER TWO

Evidence from Psychical Research

I

It is of course only possible here to select, from the mass of material in the *Proceedings of the Society for Psychical Research* and from similar scientific sources, a very few examples to illustrate the types of evidence that have been collected and the kind of problems which they raise.

These records contain a great deal of evidence of telepathy. Telepathy is the acquiring of information by modes other than that of the normal senses. It can be experimental or spontaneous. Telepathy has been observed so often that the evidence makes it extremely hard not to accept its existence.

Most early experiments in telepathy attempted to convey information of a very simple kind: cards, geometrical figures, diagrams, sense-objects of various kinds, were imagined by the agent, or else the actual objects, or drawings of them, were placed before him, and the percipient then tried to state what they were. When many experiments, following this general pattern, led to the production of positive results far beyond what could be put down to chance, it became necessary to give closer examination to whether the percipient obtained the information from the agent by some means other than by telepathy. Could the results be explained by hyperacuity of senses? When, for instance, the object to be transmitted was a playing-card on which the agent was focussing his attention, could the percipient see the image of that card reflected in the retina of the agent's eye? Or was the agent guilty, whilst he concentrated, of unconsciously whispering, which hyperacute senses in the percipient could overhear? Screening of the agent so that he should be totally invisible to the percipient was an early precaution, then the placing of the agent in a different room or building, but positive results still continued. As tests went on over the years, the precautions necessary to eliminate other explanations than that of telepathy came to reach a high degree of sophistication.

Some experimenters turned away from the methods of surrounding simple subject-matter by a complexity of precautions, and paid attention instead to increasing the complexity of the subject-matter itself. Dr. Gilbert Murray was the percipient in a very vivid and remarkable set of experiments. Here the *modus operandi* was simple, consisting of Dr. Gilbert Murray leaving the room, whilst the agent selected a subject and described it in a low voice in order that it could be written down before the experiment took place; the percipient then returned and held the hand of the agent, who was usually his daughter, Mrs. Arnold Toynbee. The experiments were carefully recorded, and some were watched by S.P.R. observers. Here is the run of four consecutive trials.

1. Subject. Mrs. Toynbee (agent). "Celia Newbolt under a gourd-tree at Smyrna."
    Professor Murray. "Modern Greek of some kind – sort of Asia Minor place – a tree and women sitting under it – a particular tree – girl sitting under it – she does not belong to the place – she is English – something to do with a poet – can't be Mrs. Kipling – no, it's a girl – rather like one of the Oliviers – don't think I can get her."
2. Subject. Mrs. Toynbee (agent). "Mr. S. playing Badminton at the Badminton Club at Bogota: Lord Murray watching, and ladies watching, one with a fan."
    Professor Murray. "This is something to do with your voyage to Panama – it's South American – it's people in white playing a game – it's your villain S. – he's playing a game – the word Bogota is coming to my mind – I think it is at a games-club."
    Mrs. Toynbee. "What is the game?"
    Professor Murray. "I think I am only guessing. I think the game is Badminton, and the Master of Elibank (Lord Murray) is there."
3. Subject. Mrs. Toynbee (agent). "I think of a scene in *Youth*, when the ship was smouldering and Marlowe is tipping up the bench because there is an explosion of gas in the hold."
    Professor Murray. "This is out of a book – it's Conrad, so I suppose it's the last Conrad I haven't read – it's a ship on fire – not exactly on fire but smouldering – a sort of stifling feeling, as if there was something underneath – it's all straining and the people don't know it – I have read it – I think it's an old Conrad – it's the story in *Youth* where they go on sailing with the ship that is burnt . . ."
4. Subject. Mrs. Toynbee (agent). "This he hasn't read – a book (of) Strindberg, called *Marriage*, about a horrid old schoolmaster I think, who goes into a restaurant and asks for female crabs to eat."
    Professor Murray. "This is a book – I haven't read it, and it's all nasty – it's a cross, tired sort of man – oh it must be Strindberg – a cross, tired sort of man going into a restaurant – he seems to be eating crabs and

tearing them up – I mean tearing them malignantly – I feel inclined to say they are female crabs but – ".*

There were 505 experiments in this Murray series, of which 167 were marked as successes, 141 as partial successes, and 197 as failures. Professor Murray himself was inclined for a time to put the results down to some unexplained kind of hyperacuity of hearing below the threshold of consciousness, though later he abandoned this theory. It will be seen that the subject-matter was far too complicated to be transmitted by any ordinary sensory methods, by signs, or by pressure of the agent's hand; how can one by such means indicate a reference to female crabs? Nor was there any drawing or other object to be read with the senses. If this is telepathy, then it can successfully pick up much more than a simple visual image, it can pick up a quite complicated mental conception.

It was soon discovered that telepathy appears to be independent of the law of the inverse square; by this law it should diminish in strength in ratio to the square of the distance between agent and percipient. Evidence suggests that it can work just as clearly from Australia as it can from the next room.

Another important aspect of telepathy emerged from the Ramsden-Miles experiments, which were carried out by two ladies, one in Scotland, the other in the south of England, who agreed that at a certain time each day one would try to send out a mental message, and the other to receive it. It was discovered that the percipient often picked up matter which was not at the time in the agent's conscious mind, but which had occupied it during the preceding twenty-four hours. This evidence for telepathy from beneath the threshold of the conscious mind of the communicator became extremely important. First, it greatly extends the possible field from which a telepathic message may take its source, for if it can be gathered from the agent's unconscious mind, how can we be sure that material is not being drawn at times by the percipient from an unconscious level in other living minds as well and not only from that of the agent? Second, it opens up the possibility that the path of telepathic communication, if it arises from the unconscious mind of the agent, may in turn pass thence directly into the unconscious mind of the percipient also, and only subsequently emerge into his conscious mind, perhaps after a time-lag; some telepathy may thus act latently. Again, what is taken for telepathy may sometimes be

* *Proc. S.P.R.*, Vol. 29, pp. 107–9.

the uprising of other latent material already long buried in the mind; it may perhaps only be the operation of latent memory, and not telepathy after all. Telepathy thus possibly becomes a very far-reaching and complicated phenomenon, to which on the one hand limits cannot safely be put, and on the other may not always be what it appears.

There is evidence also for clairvoyance, though of a less strong kind than that for telepathy, and which is hard to separate completely from it; if a percipient observes an actual physical object at a distance, or one which is present but concealed in opaque coverings, this is clairvoyance; if it is not the object itself which is observed, but only the image of it in the mind of some agent, that is telepathy. An exacting test to try and discover whether clairvoyance exists was made with the Polish medium, Ossowiecki. A drawing was made and then enclosed in opaque envelopes and carefully sealed to preclude fraudulent opening. It was sent from London to Poland by passage through several hands in order to ensure that when it reached M. Ossowiecki nobody present had ever been in contact with the one person who knew the contents of the envelope. In other words, if M. Ossowiecki were to attempt to discover the contents by telepathy instead of by clairvoyance, he had no clue as to whom in the whole world he should seek out telepathically in order to ascertain the contents. The envelope contained a drawing of a bottle with the word Swan, underlined in blue, to the left, and Ink, underlined in red, to the right. Ossowiecki reproduced the contents perfectly except that he saw them reversed from right to left. It will be noticed that the test was very skilfully devised, for it tested the power to read colour, and also included a subtle indication as to whether Ossowiecki's perception was in verbal or pictorial terms, for if the latter, he might well have *drawn* a swan. The results suggest clairvoyance, but as with most such tests it must be said that the possibility of telepathy, though much lessened, has not been excluded completely.

There also exists evidence of precognition – a good example is the apparent foreknowledge of an accident – and of retrocognition, the discovery of past happenings.

> Lady Q lived with her uncle, and dreamed he had been found dead by the side of a certain bridle-path about three miles from the house. "I knew that his horse was standing by him, and that he was wearing a dark, home-spun suit of cloth made from the wool of a herd of black sheep which he kept. I knew that his body was being brought home in a wagon with two

horses, with hay in the bottom, and that we were waiting for his body to arrive. Then in my dream the wagon came to the door; and two men well known to me – one a gardener, the other a kennel huntsman, helped to carry the body upstairs, which were rather narrow. My uncle was a very tall and heavy man, and in my dream I saw the men carrying him with difficulty, and his left hand hanging down and striking against the banisters as the men mounted the stairs. This detail gave me in my dream an unreasonable horror." Lady Q told her uncle the dream and did so again when the dream recurred two years later. Six years after the first dream, it recurred once more, and shortly after was fulfilled in every detail.*

These faculties, then, if observation of them is correct, exceed the power of the normal senses and in some cases apparently overcome the normal boundaries of space and time.

In practice it has been found convenient by modern psychical researchers to look upon these various faculties as all being branches of one faculty, grouped under the name of extra-sensory perception, or ESP.

2

Besides experimental telepathy, there is also plenty of evidence of telepathy in the field, spontaneous telepathy. Some of the best spontaneous evidence arises when, in receiving matter unknown to the percipient, it is accompanied by some striking visual appeal to the senses, in the form of a phantom, or phantasm.

Psychical research describes in general all such visions of absent persons and objects as hallucinations; the term *veridical* is applied to those hallucinations which, without implying that the absent person seen was in some way really present, yet have some sort of causal reality. Thus, if I waken in the night and see the form of my absent mother standing by my bedside there is nothing to lead me to expect it to be more than a simple hallucination, springing entirely from my own mind, but if I should see her wearing a dress of a shape and colour I have never known her to wear, and should later find that she had been wearing such a dress at the time the phantasm appeared, then, whilst still a hallucination, it would be classed as veridical or truth-bearing, for it would be supported by an objective fact. It can of course be argued that, odd though such a vision may be, it is simply due to

* *Human Personality and its Survival of Bodily Death*, by F. W. H. Myers. Abridged from Sec. 425E.

chance. It was one of the purposes of the Census of Hallucinations – a famous piece of work carried out in the early years of the S.P.R. – to estimate the odds against such visions being explicable by chance. Seventeen thousand enquiries were sent out, and nearly ten per cent produced positive answers. Where the evidence seemed good, the percipients were questioned, and confirmation sought through personal investigation by the officers of the Society. The figures then obtained were submitted to statistical examination. After making a number of exclusions, 350 apparitions of recognised living persons were reported, of which 65 were death-coincidences, the apparition occurring within twelve hours of the death of the person thus seen, the death not being known at the time to the percipient. After statistical adjustments, these latter cases were reduced to 30. The problem was whether there was a causal connection between the apparition and the death. It was reckoned that such a connection would not have occurred by chance more than once in 440 times. The statistical sample was small, and these odds are not high. The hallucinations which survived evidential sifting were classed as veridical. It still of course remained to discover how such veridical apparitions could come about.

What is striking to the student of the Census is the extreme vividness in so many cases of the phantasms when they appeared to the percipients; there is little of the half-glimpsed, the vague, the uncertain about them; brief they may be and unrepeatable, but far from being vague; on the contrary, many of them seem to have stood out as a unique and deeply impressive experience, accompanied by a clear sense of significance. It is remarkable to note how by small actions, by speaking a few words, or even in a few cases without the use of any words at all but by some apparent force of emotional transference, this significance is conveyed. The value of these cases, indeed, lies a good deal in their unexpectedness. They can make impact on the percipient without the aid of any sense of expectation on his part, indeed sometimes coming like a thunderbolt and conveying news of a totally unexpected and often disturbing kind. It seems possible in some of these spontaneous cases that occasions of acute emotional intensity in the agent – perhaps never to be repeated in a lifetime – may arouse in the percipient a normally dim or totally obscured telepathic faculty to a momentary clarity, during which the perception is registered.

In general the evidence in the Census suggests that many veridical phantasms may arise from a projection of thought, which, as in some telepathic experiments, is initiated by the agent, is received by the percipient's unconscious mind, and then emerges into his conscious mind by a process by which he himself creates the phantasmal image. The agent may send the impulse, but the percipient, so to speak, clothes it; it is therefore partly subjective in presentation. This would account for the element of incompleteness sometimes found in the telepathic image as received, perhaps the appearance only of the head and upper part of the body, and also for the element of added detail, such as when Canon Bourne's niece saw his apparition, including that of his horse, in the hunting field, and noticed the Lincoln Bennett label in his hat when he waved it, though with normal vision it would have been quite impossible to see it at the distance.

Sometimes the agent acquires information at a distance; in this it resembles some cases of clairvoyance; a few cases suggest the possibility that the consciousness of the agent in some way may be able to travel, and in part at least to accompany its own phantasm. Mr. C. R. Wilmot writes:

> On October 3rd, 1863, I sailed from Liverpool for New York . . . On the evening of the second day out . . . a severe storm began, which lasted for nine days . . . Upon the night following the eighth day of the storm . . . I dreamed that I saw my wife, whom I had left in the United States, come to the door of my state-room, clad in her nightdress. At the door she seemed to discover that I was not the only occupant of the room, hesitated a little, then advanced to my side, stooped down and kissed me, and after gently caressing me for a few moments, quietly withdrew. Upon waking I was surprised to see my fellow-passenger, whose berth was above mine, but not directly over it – owing to the fact that our room was at the stern of the vessel – leaning upon his elbow, and looking fixedly at me. "You're a pretty fellow", said he at length, "to have a lady come and visit you in this way." I pressed him for an explanation, which he at first declined to give, but at length related what he had seen while wide awake, lying in his berth. It exactly corresponded with my dream . . . The day after landing . . . almost (my wife's) first question when we were alone together was "Did you receive a visit from me a week ago Tuesday?" . . . On the . . . same night when . . . the storm had just begun to abate, she had lain awake for a long time thinking of me, and about four o'clock in the morning it seemed to her that she went out to seek me. Crossing the wide and stormy sea, she came at length to a low, black steamship, whose side she went up, and then descending into the cabin, passed through it to the stern until she came to my state-room. "Tell me," she said, "do they ever have state-rooms like the one I saw, where the upper berth extends further back than the under one? A man was in the upper berth, looking right at me, and for a moment I was

afraid to go in, but soon I went up to the side of your berth, bent down and kissed you, and embraced you, and then went away . . ."*

Mr. Wilmot's sister was also on the voyage, and confirmed that she had been asked next morning by her brother's state-room companion, Mr. Tait, if she had been in to see him. It is interesting to note that whilst Mr. Wilmot *dreamed* the vision of Mrs. Wilmot, his companion in the cabin saw it whilst *awake*. Mrs. Wilmot's account of seeming to cross the stormy sea may of course largely consist of subjective imagery.

If Mrs. Wilmot had merely been in telepathic communication with her husband, and acting as the agent, it is doubtful whether she would have become aware of the third party in the cabin. And could the third party have become aware of her, if the vision were entirely a subjective presentation in Mr. Wilmot's mind? The theory has been put forward that Mr. Wilmot, after first being the recipient, then also acted as agent, and relayed the image onward in turn to his companion, who perceived it indirectly through him, and the phantasm was thus subjectively constructed, in turn, by the companion. This, however unlikely, may be the safest thing to assume. But, although the facts do not compel it, it is hard to reject the possibility altogether that Mrs. Wilmot's consciousness may in some degree have been present in that cabin. If so, what degree of objectivity are we to allow to that dissociated image, when her actual body was lying in bed all the while a very long distance away?

These cases of phantasms are very far from uniform, varying greatly in the degree of subjectivity, in the amount of apparent participation by the agent, and in their general significance. Many coincide, or nearly coincide, with some moment of crisis. Others appear to be almost pointless. Most are seen only by one person, a few are collective, or seen independently in quick succession by more than one percipient. There are also cases of the successful experimental projection of a phantasm of himself by a living person. A phantasm, in taking on the appearance of a certain person, often does so, as we have seen, with a certain degree of incompleteness; and although the initiating impulse possibly originates more often than not in the person whose image it presents, we are very uncertain of the respective parts played by the agent and the percipient in the selective shaping of the image.

* *Human Personality*, 666C.

Now a large number of these phantasms appear, as far as can be ascertained, at or very near to the moment of the death of the persons they represent. We begin to find ourselves on the borderline between life and death. Between the one case and the next, between phantasms of the living and of the dead, there is no real break. The cases shade imperceptibly into one another. It is very important to find out as much as possible about ESP between the living and how it operates, otherwise it would be easy to attribute to telepathy from the dead what may really be telepathy from the living.

N. T. Menneer, principal of Torre College, Torquay, wrote in 1883:

> My wife, since deceased, had a brother residing at Sarawak, and staying with the Raja, Sir James Brooke . . . Mr. Wellington (my wife's brother) was killed in a brave attempt to defend Mrs. Middleton and her children. The Chinese, it appears, taking Mr. Wellington for the Raja's son, struck off his head.
>
> And now for the dream. I was awoke one night by my wife, who started from her sleep, terrified by the following dream. She saw her headless brother standing at the foot of the bed with his head lying on a coffin by his side . . . At length she fell asleep again, to be awoke by a similar dream. In the morning, and for several days after, she constantly referred to her dream, and anticipated sad news of her brother.*

The psychical researcher, Gurney, commented that "this dream, if it is to be telepathically explained, must apparently have been due to the last flash of thought in the brother's consciousness. It may seem strange that a definite picture of his mode of death should present itself to a man in the instant of receiving an unexpected and fatal blow; but, as Hobbes said, 'thought is quick'."

Gurney's argument shows how hard it is sometimes to be sure that a phantasm at the time it is projected is that of a dead and not a dying person, that it has not been conveyed telepathically before death and has lain latent in the percipient's unconscious mind, only emerging later after the death had taken place.

What of a case where a phantasm appears and conveys news of the death of another person to a percipient who does not yet know of it? Miss Dodson writes:

> On June 5th, 1887 . . . between 11 and 12 at night, being awake, my name was called three times. I answered twice, thinking it was my uncle, "Come in,

* *Human Personality*, 429A.

Uncle George, I am awake," but the third time I recognised the voice as that of my mother, who had been dead sixteen years. I said, "Mamma!" She then came round a screen near my bedside with two children in her arms and placed them in my arms and put the bedclothes over them and said, "Lucy, *promise* me to take care of them." I replied, "Yes, I promise you"; and I added, "Oh, mamma, stay and speak to me, I am so wretched." She replied, "Not yet, my child," then she seemed to go round the screen again, and I remained, feeling the children to be still in my arms, and fell asleep. When I awoke there was nothing. Tuesday morning, June 7th, I received the news of my sister-in-law's death. She had given birth to a child three weeks before, which I did not know till after her death."*

On examination, Miss Dodson stated that she was in no anxiety about her sister-in-law, did not know that a second baby had been born, did not know her sister-in-law was ill, and could not imagine whose children could have seemed to have been placed in her arms.

It is hard to be sure that it was one of the two dead persons concerned who brought the news, and not the living percipient who by some mode of telepathy initiated the discovery for herself, and then herself externalised the facts thus discovered into a phantasmal image of her mother. Such is the roundabout explanation which the caution of the researcher is likely to prefer. Yet it is also necessary to ask who or what directed the percipient's attention to the dead or dying person just at that very time. It is hard indeed to conceive of a telepathic faculty in a living person keeping a kind of continual watch upon the persons best known to its owner. These cases would be so very much easier if we could accept that the obvious motives which appear to direct many of them are really operative, but science has to be far more cautious than this, as the following case also shows.

... Michael Conley, a farmer living near Ionia, Chickasaw County, was found dead in an outhouse ... The old clothes which he wore were covered with filth from the place where he was found, and they were thrown outside the morgue on the ground. His son came from Ionia, and took the corpse home. When he reached there, and one of the daughters was told that her father was dead, she fell into a swoon ... When at last she was brought from the swoon, she said: "Where are father's old clothes? He has just appeared to me dressed in a white shirt, black clothes, and felt (misreported for satin) slippers, and told me that after leaving home he sewed a large roll of bills inside his grey shirt with a piece of my red dress, and the money is still there ..." The young man ... told Coroner Hoffmann what his sister had said. Mr. Hoffman admitted that the lady had described the identical burial garb in which her father was clad, even to the slippers, although she never

* *Human Personality*, 718A.

saw him after death, and none of the family had seen more than his face through the coffin lid. Curiosity being fully aroused, they took the grey shirt from the bundle, and within the bosom found a large roll of bills sewed with a piece of red cloth. The young man said his sister had a red dress exactly like it. The stitches were large and irregular, and looked to be those of a man.*

The story was corroborated by the Coroner and the local pastor. The roll contained thirty-five dollars.

Several of the well-known problems of evidence of extra-sensory perception crop up in this case. Who initiated the conveying of the knowledge of the money, a fact known by the dead person, but not, as far as has been discovered, by any living person? If initiated by Michael Conley, was it immediately before he died? If so, would he have been likely to convey an image of himself in his funeral clothes? If by the daughter, did she really discover the facts clairvoyantly during her swoon, and then represent it to her conscious mind by creating an image of her father speaking to her? If she saw clairvoyantly, why did she not see the coat, with the stitching, or the roll of money itself, instead of *hearing* about it from her father's image? If Conley initiated the image after his death, thus demonstrating some form of survival, did he have a first-hand knowledge, or only an inferential one, of the clothing in which his dead body had been clad? Did he after death project some kind of thought-image of himself, which his daughter re-interpreted subjectively? On the other hand, if his appearance was in some way objective, was there any degree of objectivity in the *clothes* she saw him wearing? It can be seen what caution is needed in investigating these cases.

4

The difficulty in nearly all spontaneous cases is that they are so brief, though often vivid. They are largely single unrepeated experiences, and are already past and over before we can begin to investigate them. We have to accept the few facts they contain and cannot add to them.

An entirely different situation arises when mediums, whether professional or amateur, set out with the purpose of deliberate and sustained communication with the dead. They seek to present, and are judged by, a far more extended and richer field of evidence than can be found in spontaneous cases: a great deal more is expected of them.

* *Human Personality*, 721.

The enquirer will demand a number of things of the facts offered by mediums in evidence of survival: that they must be purposive facts, and not ones which, even if correct, are lacking in any significance; that they exhibit behind them a mind which is working towards an intelligible aim, and which displays a range of facts known to the alleged survivor. It is expected that the facts should be grouped and presented with the particular emotional and intellectual significance which they bore to the dead person: in other words, with that especial flavour and selectiveness which expresses his own personality and influences and colours his choice of facts. Let us say that a son receives communications purporting to be from his dead father. The two will share many memories in common, but the facts chosen by the father will be expected to reflect a different aspect; for instance, they may show knowledge of the lady who in the sitter's mind and emotions is his mother, but who to the father is his wife. If the medium were to tap by telepathy, consciously or unconsciously, the memory of the living son, the sitter, the image to be read might be expected to be that of the mother, not of the wife. Where evidence is strong in facts, but weak in this personal flavour, it is always more open to be explained as telepathy from the living.

We ask of the evidence, therefore, that the facts presented are not isolated ones, but are embedded in material which expresses as much as possible of the characteristics of the deceased – in short, we seek evidence of *identity*. We also ask of the facts that they shall not be merely random, vague, and without meaning and coherence; we require them to show evidence of *purpose*.

With mediumistic communications, then, we are no longer concerned with the brief telepathic impact, but with deliberate and sustained two-way conversation, with opportunities for question and answer. We want to establish whether the personality of a dead person can contact us in its fullness, and continue to do so.

5

Has evidence been obtained by the S.P.R. which goes some way towards being able to satisfy these requirements?

"George Pelham", born an American but a member of the English nobility, a man engaged in literature and philosophy, met an early death in February 1892, from a fall. It was purported that he then made communications through a trance medium, Mrs. Piper, all of whose work was throughout the time of the G.P. appearances under the direct control of an S.P.R. investigator, Dr. Richard Hodgson, whose summary follows. Care was taken that the names of the sitters concerned were not disclosed to Mrs. Piper.

On the first appearance of the communicating G.P. to Mr. Hart in March 1892, he gave not only his own name and that of the sitter, but also the names of several of their most intimate common friends, and referred specifically to the most important private matters connected with them. At the same sitting reference was made to other incidents unknown to the sitters, such as the account of Mrs. Pelham's taking the studs from the body of G.P. and giving them to Mr. Pelham to be sent to Mr. Hart, and the reproduction of a notable remembrance of a conversation which G.P. living had with Katherine, the daughter of his most intimate friends, the Howards. These were primary examples of two kinds of knowledge concerning matters unknown to the sitters, of which various other instances were afterwards given; knowledge of events connected with G.P. which had occurred since his death, and knowledge of special memories pertaining to the G.P. personality before death. A week later, at the sitting of Mr. Vance, he made an appropriate inquiry after the sitter's son, and in reply to inquiries rightly specified that the sitter's son had been at college with him and further gave a correct description of the sitter's summer home as the place of a special visit. This, again, was paralleled by many later instances where appropriate inquiries were made and remembrances recalled concerning other personal friends of G.P. Nearly two weeks later came his most intimate friends, the Howards, and to these, using the voice directly, he showed such a fullness of private remembrance and specific knowledge and characteristic intellectual and emotional quality pertaining to G.P. that, though they had previously taken no interest in any branch of psychical research, they were unable to resist the conviction that they were actually conversing with their old friend G.P. And this conviction was strengthened by their later experiences. Not least important, at that time, was his anxiety about the disposal of a certain book and about certain specified letters which concerned matters too private for publication. He was particularly desirious of convincing his father, who lived in Washington, that it was indeed G.P. who was communicating, and he soon afterwards stated that his father had taken his photograph to be copied, as was the case, though Mr. Pelham had not informed even his wife of this fact. Later on he reproduced a series of incidents, unknown to the sitters, in which Mrs. Howard had been engaged in her own home. Later still, at a sitting with his father and mother in New York, a further intimate knowledge was shown of private family circumstances, and at the following sitting, at which his father and mother were not present, he gave the details of certain private actions which they had done in the interim. At their sitting, and at various sittings of the Howards, appropriate comments were made concerning different articles presented which had belonged to G.P. living, or had been familiar to him; he inquired after other personal articles which were not presented at the sittings, and showed intimate and detailed recollections of incidents in connection with them. In points connected with the recognition of articles with their related associations of a personal sort, the G.P. communicating, so far as I know, has never failed. Nor has he failed in the recognition of personal friends. I may say generally that out of a large number of sitters who went as strangers to Mrs. Piper, the communicating G.P. has picked out the friends of G.P. living, precisely as the G.P. living might have been expected to do (thirty cases of recognition out of at least one hundred and fifty persons who have had sittings with Mrs. Piper since the first appearance of G.P., and no case of false recognition), and has exhibited memories in connection with these and other friends which are such as would naturally be associated as part of the G.P. personality, which certainly do not suggest in themselves that they originate otherwise, and which are accompanied by the emotional relations which were connected with such friends in the mind of G.P. living . . . The manifestations of this G.P. communicating have not been of a fitful and spasmodic nature, they have exhibited the marks of a continuous living and persistent personality, manifesting itself through a course of years, and showing the same characteristics of an independent intelligence whether friends of G.P. were present at the sittings or not. I learned of various cases where in my absence active assistance was rendered by G.P. to sitters who had never previously heard of him, and from time to time he would make brief pertinent reference to matters with which G.P. living was acquainted, though I was not, and sometimes in ways which indicated that he could to some extent see what was happening in our world to persons in whose welfare G.P. living would have been specially interested.*

The G.P. case is probably the best of its kind in the S.P.R. records. In the field of psychical research the excellence of any case can never be better than the excellence of the *record* of it; if the record is poor, the case becomes poor also. This is the weakness of most Spiritualistic cases. The care and sustained attention given to the G.P. case is an essential part of its value.

The strength of this case is considered by most minds to lie in the way in which the evidence is spread over a considerable number of people. Some other minds consider that a case may be stronger if the evidence for it is, on the contrary, limited to a few facts only. They argue that because the facts are few they can be examined more narrowly and certainty more easily reached about them, and also that there is less margin for alternative explanations. The ideal case, from

---

* *Proc.*, Vol. 13, p. 328.

this point of view, should approach as nearly as possible to having but one single and decisive fact.

The Pearl Tie-Pin Case

Miss C., the sitter, has a cousin, an officer with our Army in France, who was killed in battle a month previously to the sitting; this she knew. One day, after the name of her cousin had unexpectedly been spelt out on the ouija board and her name given in answer to her query: "Do you know who I am?" the following message came: "Tell mother to give my pearl tie-pin to the girl I was going to marry, I think she ought to have it." When asked what was the name and address of the lady, both were given, the name spelt out included the full Christian and surname, the latter being a very unusual one and quite unknown to both the sitters. The address given in London was either fictitious or taken down incorrectly, as a letter sent there was returned and the whole message was thought to be fictitious. Six months later, however, it was discovered that the officer had been engaged, shortly before he left for the front, to the very lady whose name was given; he had however told no one. Neither his cousin nor any of his own family in Ireland were aware of the fact, and had never seen the lady nor heard her name, until the War Office sent over the deceased officer's effects. Then they found that he had put this lady's name in his will as his next of kin, both Christian and surname being precisely the same as given through the automatist; and what is equally remarkable, a pearl tie-pin was found in his effects. Both the ladies have signed a document . . . affirming the accuracy of the above. The message was recorded at the time, and not written from memory after verification had been obtained.*

The Case of the Shark

The Australian banker, Hugh Junor Browne . . . had the misfortune to lose his two sons during a cruise they were making in their yacht . . . The parents were very anxious when their sons did not return, and applied for information to the . . . medium . . . George Sprigg . . . One of Mr. Browne's sons manifested through the medium's mouth, furnishing . . . details of the drama, among them the tragic particular that his brother's body had been mutilated of an arm by a shark. This was confirmed in an extraordinary manner, for a shark was caught in whose stomach Hugh's arm was found, together with a piece of his waistcoat, his watch and a few coins. The watch had stopped at nine o'clock, the hour indicated by the medium as that when the shipwreck took place.†

When a telepathic explanation is sought for, as it first must be, it is not easy to formulate in whose mind the facts in these two cases could

* *On the Threshold of the Unseen* (Sir W. Barrett), p. 184.
† *Discarnate Influence in Human Life* (Professor Bozzano), p. 219.

have been present, at the time they were given, other than the mind of the dead person from which they purport to come. Psychical research, however, as we shall see, can by no means move towards a hypothesis of survival as easily and quickly as these cases may seem to indicate it might.

CHAPTER THREE

Hypotheses Pointing Away from Survival

I

IN THE fifty-odd volumes of the *Proceedings of the Society for Psychical Research* are to be found many hundreds of pages of closely scrutinised evidence of survival of death, some of it, as we have seen in the G.P. case, of considerable consistency and vividness, other parts of it variable and poor or uncertain in quality. In *Proceedings* also are thousands of pages which represent honourable attempts on the part of psychical researchers to provide alternative explanations of this evidence, for scientific caution requires that hypotheses which can explain the evidence in terms of facts related to this world must always be preferred to a hypothesis of survival, unless overwhelming evidence requires the latter to be accepted. Therefore the duty of psychical research has been to take these apparent facts which it has collected, and to go on to ask if they do not necessarily point to survival at all, but can be explained in terms of living human experience, ordinary or abnormal, without having to draw upon any factors outside our present life. Besides looking for such external explanations, as one might name them, psychical research has also the duty of scrutinising the evidence internally and asking whether, in so far as it points to survival, it raises at the same time anomalies and self-contradictions which destroy its claims from within. Both these sorts of questions must precede any setting-up of a working hypothesis of survival.

Let us look at the first class, at the principal alternative explanations of an external kind which have been put forward to account for the phenomena observed.

Fraud

This is the simplest and most obvious explanation which if always true would then leave no new facts for science to consider. It has long been hard for an investigator to consider that fraud can be held to account for all the phenomena examined. Fraud has been detected a number of times and strongly suspected at others. However there are many other cases in the field of mental phenomena where there is no evidence to suggest that fraud has arisen. Whether these cases necessarily suggest survival is of course a different matter. Very careful precautions have been taken at times in order to produce conditions where the practice of fraud would be almost impossible or, if present, highly likely to be detected.

Mrs. Piper, for many years under very complete supervision by her investigators, provided for long a test case. Suitable medical tests were made on her whilst in her trance state – pricking of the skin, the application of strongly flavoured articles to the tongue, inspection of the eye-balls by rolling-up of the eyelids – and her trance was found to be cataleptic, that is, she was unconscious of what was proceeding around her. The mind, whether it was her own or that of a discarnate being, or both, whether functioning separately or together, which operated in her during this trance frequently attempted "fishing", the extraction of information from the sitter by questioning, or by picking up any inferences available from whatever was said. Fishing was excluded by developing a technique of non-committal remarks by the sitters; it was then found that extra-sensory facts were as easily produced without fishing. Could however the trance mind of Mrs. Piper make available to itself facts discovered at other times by Mrs. Piper's normal mind, either by ordinary observation or by deliberately fraudulent means? The practice was made of excluding from Mrs. Piper all possible knowledge of her sitters, by keeping them anonymous, by never allowing her to see from one year to another the written record of the sittings, and by not allowing her sitters to enter her presence until she was already in the trance state and therefore unconscious of them. Dr. Hyslop, a careful investigator, even went so far as to wear a mask at early sittings, until so much evidence of his identity was produced during trance that to wear it became pointless. Dr. Hodgson, in whose hands was placed the general conduct of the investigation of Mrs. Piper's mediumship, once rebuked a sitter for leaving a wet umbrella in the hall-stand. "How am I to know," he asked angrily, "that you have not slipped a note inside it offering information which will be picked up, handed by a confederate to Mrs. Piper after we have left, and reproduced in the trance state next time you come?" Another sort of test was devised by Oliver Lodge. Mrs. Piper was invited to his home on a visit and given ample opportunity of finding out all she could about him and his numerous family by ordinary means, of which to all appearances she did not avail herself. At sittings she produced information alleged to be from a dead uncle of Oliver Lodge, giving facts the latter could not remember ever having heard concerning this uncle's boyhood. Oliver Lodge then employed a private detective, placed all the facts given in trance at his disposal, and asked him by enquiries on the spot and by other ordinary professional methods to see if he could find out the same facts independently. His report was that Mrs. Piper, without the freedom of movement he enjoyed, had done a great deal better than he was able to.

Whilst, then, most psychical researchers are in general satisfied where mental phenomena are concerned, that fraud is not an explanation which will cover all the facts, they necessarily have to remain constantly alive to its possibilities.

Co-incidence

The hypothesis of co-incidence is based on the supposition that we remember the remarkable cases and forget all about the dreams and apparitions and fancies that are not veridical, and that if these were counted in as well, the net result would not exceed what could be put down to chance. Co-incidence becomes stronger as an explanation when evidence of purpose in an alleged communicator is weak and lacking; and vice versa. When out of 150 persons who sat with Mrs. Piper, the G.P. entity picked out 30 whom the living G.P. had known, and none whom he had not, clearly something other than co-incidence is at work.

Co-incidence as a hypothesis is destroyed, as Bergson has pointed out, if only one case is produced which cannot possibly be attributed to chance. The co-incidence hypothesis remains a useful but limited weapon in the armoury of the researcher for weeding out some of the weaker cases, especially cases of single and isolated statements.

Hypnosis

Extra-sensory powers have often been observed when a subject is under hypnotic trance. Hypnosis is now usually considered to be in essence a process of self-suggestion, aided by the hypnotist, but not produced by imposing his "will" upon the subject. It can be a mode of bringing up the contents of the unconscious mind to the surface by inducing in the subject a state of dissociation from the normal mind. In hypnosis information is sometimes produced which is apparently derived clairvoyantly or telepathically.

Hypnosis thus sometimes accompanies cases of extra-sensory perception.

The problem implicit in hypnosis, considered from the viewpoint of psychical research, is not whether it is the cause of ESP; obviously it is not, for though it accompanies some cases of ESP, it is absent from many others; the problem is how far dissociation of some kind, of which hypnosis is an experimentally-induced type, is an essential factor in releasing powers of ESP, whether hypnotism can throw light on the processes by which a mind can actively gather, or passively receive, information not normally accessible to it. How far this is possible, and whether only from living minds, or from the minds of the dead also, is a matter of evidence. An entranced medium sometimes answers questions from the sitter and produces extra-sensory information in a way very closely resembling that in which hypnotised subjects answer their hypnotists, and may as readily respond to false suggestions put to her. The dissociated medium may therefore really be drawing much more from the sitter than is purported, could at times indeed be little more than a mirror reflecting some of the contents of his mind. In other words the entranced medium may not be representing the alleged communicator but only the sitter's memories of him. If material is produced which is not consciously known to the sitter, where has it been drawn from? This question is precisely the same one which arises in extended telepathy, which is described below.

Secondary and Multiple Personality

There are medical cases of multiple personality - Sally Beauchamp, Leonie, and "Eve" are well-known ones - in which ESP phenomena have shown themselves spasmodically. The problem these cases raise is whether trance control of a medium is a phenomenon of the same kind, in which no more is involved than a dramatic presentation of a split-off part or parts of the medium's own personality.

We have here one of the most complex of the many problems relating to mediumship. How far may such trance personalities spring partly or wholly from the unconscious, and be representations of the archetypal figures described by Jung, or other hidden aspects of the medium's personality? This is a profoundly difficult problem.

It is easy for comparisons of the trance-mediumship state with that of medically observed cases of split personality to become almost exclusively occupied in considering whether, since the latter clearly spring from deep disturbances of personality, trance mediumship is similarly based on neurotic impulses. What when trance mediumship arises in an otherwise psychologically healthy and well-ordered personality? It is easy to make an assumption that a trance state *per se* is neurotic. It has to be discovered whether it is so or not by its fruits.

Dissociated aspects of a multiple personality can oppose one another – as they are often seen to do in the medically observed cases – and struggle for possession of the conscious field of the personality. The latter is then full of disorder. So, often, are the dissociated aspects taking part in the struggle, although at times a secondary aspect can be more orderly than the normal personality. However the dissociation itself points to disorder somewhere in the total personality. Where a dissociated personality appears through the mediumistic trance, works in harmonious association with the normal conscious aims of the medium, and returns and withdraws at stated times and in an orderly manner, and if the trance personality, when it exercises ESP faculties, performs its task towards the medium's sitters in an orderly way – then although this does not prove that the trance personality is necessarily more than another aspect of the medium, it is hard to see where any fundamental disorder is to be found, unless we are prepared to attribute disorder to the trance process itself.

The problem before psychical research is whether the trance personality behaves so much like medically observed secondary personalities as to eliminate the need for any other hypothesis or whether it has quite distinctive features of its own. It has to ask whether this trance personality, if it is what it claims to be, is obliged to use something of the same processes (whatever these may be) of obtaining temporary domination over the normal personality, as take place when a secondary personality appears in neurotic patients. This problem is further complicated when the trance personalities are no childish messenger or fatherly guide who can readily be conceived as holding a psychologically suitable relationship to the medium's normal personality, but on the contrary claim to be relatives or friends of the sitter, and produce evidence appropriate to the personalities they claim to be.

No causal relationship has ever been shown to exist, for instance, between Mrs. Piper and the G.P. personality, and would the latter have ever appeared had not G.P.'s friends chosen to attend seances? From whose need, then, is such a personality or pseudo-personality projected – the medium's or the sitter's? If the latter, it is very hard to see how the G.P. figure can properly be regarded as a secondary personality of Mrs. Piper's.

It has to be admitted that the use so far made in psychical research of medical cases of multiple personality has been almost entirely limited to considering these as a counter-hypothesis to evidence of survival. No full-scale study has yet been made of the characteristics of different types of trance personalities or pseudo-personalities as seen in mediumship.

Cosmic Mind

If survival is to be excluded, then the alternative sometimes demands such extraordinary powers of gathering information on the part of the unconscious mind of the medium that it has been postulated that the latter could only obtain its knowledge from some cosmic reservoir of facts, or even from some cosmic mind, wherein all facts, important and trivial, past and present, are alike stored and available for instant perception. It need hardly be said that no scientist propounds this theory seriously; it has merely been set forth by researchers as a possibility, to be mentioned for the sake of completeness, and then dismissed.

The Extended Telepathy Theory

Extended telepathy, or super telepathy, between the living is the important alternative explanation to that of survival. We know that the giving at a seance of facts which are not in the sitter's conscious mind is no proof at all that telepathy from the living can be excluded as an explanation. For the Ramsden-Miles experiments have shown that telepathy has, at any rate at times, the power of acquiring knowledge which has been in the sitter's mind, but of which he is not at that moment conscious.

The telepathic theory is then extended to say that one cannot exclude the possibility that anything whatever which a person has ever thought or known is still lying submerged in his or her unconscious or subliminal mind, and can pass thence to a medium without the owner of this knowledge being aware of it. Theoretically this must include the most casual scraps of information, gleaned only perhaps from an odd glance at a stranger's newspaper many years before.

Next it is further assumed as a possibility that the contents of the minds of *other* living persons as well as the sitter's may be accessible to the medium or percipient, who can then find and extract facts from it at will, even if the sensitive has no conscious knowledge of so doing, and does not even know of the existence or whereabouts of the living person bearing that information.

Now there *are* a few very remarkable examples of a living mind obtaining information from another living mind, not in a random way, but in a way closely resembling, even in the sort of mistakes made, the manner in which a medium claims to receive them from the dead.

William Stead was in the habit of using automatic writing – that is, he allowed his hand to write of itself without providing it consciously with any thoughts to express – in order to obtain information, unknown to his conscious mind, from living friends concerning their recent activities:

> A friend of mine . . . had spent the week-end at Haslemere, thirty miles rom London. She was to lunch with me on the Wednesday, if she had returned to town. On the Monday afternoon I wished to know about this, so taking up a pen I asked the lady mentally if she had returned home. My hand wrote as follows: "I am sorry to say that I have had a most unpleasant experience, which I am almost ashamed to tell you. I left Haslemere at 2.27 p.m. in a second-class compartment, in which were two women and a man. At Godalming the women got out and I was left alone with the man. He came over and sat by me. I was alarmed and pushed him away. He would not move, however, and tried to kiss me. I was furious and there was a struggle, during which I seized his umbrella and struck him with it repeatedly, but it broke, and I was afraid I should get the worst of it, when the train stopped at some distance from Guildford. The man took fright, left me before the train reached the station, jumped out and took to his heels. I was extremely agitated, but I kept the umbrella." I sent my secretary immediately to the lady's house, with a note in which I expressed my regret for the assault she had suffered, adding: "Calm yourself, and bring me the man's umbrella on Wednesday." She replied: "I am sorry you have learnt of what happened to me, because I had decided not to speak of it to anyone; but the umbrella was mine, not his."★

Professor Bozzano quotes from Doctor Soal's summary of the remarkable Gordon Davis case.

★ *Discarnate Influence in Human Life* (Professor Bozzano), p. 57.

It is a case in which a person, believed by the sitter to be dead, communicates spontaneously through the direct voice. He reproduces more or less accurately the tone of his voice, its accent and his characteristic mannerisms of speech. He describes incidents of his boyhood known to the sitter and speaks of one or two matters unknown to the sitter. Most interesting of all, he gives an accurate description of the environment and interior arrangements of a house which he did not occupy until a year later. Going back into the past he is able to reproduce accurately the place of his last meeting with the sitter and the substance of the conversation. Further, he is dramatized as if he were a deceased personality, desiring to send messages of comfort to his wife and child. In the end we discover that he is still living. By means of a diary kept by him, we are able to discover accurately just what he was doing at the time of the first two sittings . . . He was in his own office occupied in discussing business with his clients . . . This dramatized personality, so accurate in its other statements, apparently believes itself to be a deceased person. We might, of course, assume that this idea was suggested to it by the spiritistic mind of the medium, who in turn obtained false information from the mind of the sitter. But is this the true explanation? It is to be noted that Gordon Davis does not give any details about the circumstances of his death.*

On another occasion, Professor Soal invents a fictitious friend whom he names "Ferguson", and later on details he has invented about him are given back to him by a medium.

In these cases we have the problem of the process of initiation. Did Stead's mind, and that of Soal's medium, Mrs. Cooper, go forth and obtain the information, or did these minds merely remain receptive, the information being actively imparted to them by the subliminal minds of those to whom the facts related, i.e. the lady in the train, and the still-living Gordon Davis? Did Soal's mind, when he was the sitter, impinge the "Ferguson" details upon the medium, or did she rifle them from his mind by her own unconscious initiative? Or is it in some way a mutual process? Whatever the process, the important question is whether *all* information purporting to proceed from the dead is really no more than a presentation, in deceiving form, of facts having their origin in living minds, which was clearly their origin in these three cases, though we have no satisfactory way of accounting for how the transfer of information came about? It is plain that psychical research cannot accept the hypothesis of survival so long as the evidence can still be assumed to be explicable *entirely* by causes within living minds.

* *Proc.*, vol. 35, and *Discarnate Influence in Human Life* (Professor Bozzano), pp. 83–4.

This it endeavours to do with the help of the extended telepathy theory.

Three serious weaknesses show themselves in this theory. The first weakness is that if a medium has this wide power of gathering facts at will from the minds of living persons present at the time, or even from others totally unknown to her, this super-telepathy still cannot explain at all how the facts are *selected*. How is the medium able to step with even partial success into the shoes of the discarnate alleged communicator, and make much the sort of selection of material which would prove appropriate to the contents of his mind and memory, and sometimes to his emotions as well? How can she pick some of these facts, and presumably reject thousands of others which under this theory must be held to be equally accessible to her from other minds? In the Pearl Tie-pin case, for instance, how was the medium enabled to select correctly the name of the dead officer's fiancee; if she obtained it from the lady herself – a living person unknown both to sitter and medium – who or what directed the medium's mind to that lady in the first place?*

The second weakness is that if the subliminal mind really does possess these very extensive powers, why have they not long since been discovered and harnessed to useful ends? The remarkable quality of the power does not match its application; it is strange if a power which far exceeds man's normal perceptions arises largely in order to deceive him, which indeed reaches its richest flowering when engaged in deceit, that is, when giving messages from the dead which are really not from the dead at all.

If mediumship is no more than a faculty for the tapping of knowledge, by telepathy from the living, or by the clairvoyant perception of objects or written records, then those who believe this to be the best hypothesis should surely set about getting mediums to obtain knowledge of this wide and immediate kind, set about getting the channel to run clear without impersonation of the dead, without any reference to survival at all. On the other hand, if this ready apprehension of mental or recorded fact from diverse sources, this subliminal filching, is a myth, if little direct evidence without reference to the survival evidence can be established, then it is probable it will eventually have to be eliminated as an explanation of every case of purported survival.

* The selectivity argument is very well reasoned by C. J. Ducasse in *Journal S.P.R.*, Dec. 1962, pp. 401-6.

The third weakness in the extended telepathy theory is that it does not satisfactorily account for how the subliminal mind, conceived as being able to obtain such accurate information from the mind of the living, should not frequently have some knowledge, however imperfect, of the *sources* of its information and be able constantly to name the *living* minds from which it has drawn it, as Stead was able to, when he consciously attempted to reach the living mind of his friend.

It is of course the case that an entirely different standard of evidence is being applied by researchers – perfectly legitimately – to the extended telepathy theory from that which is applied to the hypothesis of survival. This is necessary for a time, because, as has been said, scientific integrity must prefer every rival claim to the survival hypothesis as long as it legitimately can. Evidence for extended telepathy has to be considered very seriously although it forms no more than a theoretical possibility; evidence for survival has to be rejected even when it forms quite a strong probability. The extended telepathy theory is therefore one of admitted extravagance. Its strength consists in its being a necessary and cautious form of *criticism* of the survival hypothesis; it has never become a *working* hypothesis existing in its own right and on its own merits. It is because the facts make the survival theory hard to dispose of, or rather that a part of the facts do so, that the extended telepathy theory has had to remain for so long a theoretical possibility, in order that it may still bear the burden of explaining some of the facts which would otherwise need to be explained by the survival hypothesis. The stronger the survival evidence, the more extravagant the extended telepathy theory needs to become. It is so far a negative theory, an artificial concept. Eventually a point might be reached where extended telepathy cannot reasonably support the burden it is asked to carry. It would then be necessary to set up a working hypothesis of survival, or else to work upon yet another alternative theory.

Let us apply it to a particular case, an old and not very important one, and one not fully documented, but which serves well as an illustration of what is involved. The Rev. M'Kay, a Catholic priest, writes on October 21st, 1842, to the Countess of Shrewsbury:

> In July 1838 on my arrival in Perth I was called upon by a Presbyterian woman, Anne Simpson, who for more than a week had been in the utmost anxiety to see a priest. This woman stated that a woman lately dead (date not given) named Maloy, slightly known to Anne Simpson, had "appeared to her during the night for several nights," urging her to go to the priest,

who would pay a sum of money, three and tenpence, which the deceased owed to a person not specified. I made enquiry, and found that a woman of that name had died, who had acted as washerwoman and followed the regiment. Following up the enquiry I found a grocer with whom she had dealt, and on asking if a female named Maloy owed him anything, he turned up his books, and told me she did owe him three and tenpence. I paid the sum. Subsequently the Presbyterian woman came to me, saying that she was no more troubled.*

If the theory of survival is to be rejected and the extended telepathy theory applied to this case, then these happenings must be supposed to have been activated by the subliminal mind of the only living person who so far as the evidence allows us to judge is known to have been aware of the debt – the creditor. It is then necessary to suppose that this subliminal mind of the tradesman, on the alert for possible bad debts and keeping a constant eye on his list of customers, gets to know subliminally of the death of one, wonders how to collect the debt, ranges the world of unknown persons till he finds a friend of the deceased, influences her telepathically by himself directly or indirectly creating a phantasm of the dead person, and thus gets his debt of 3s. 10d. repaid, to the satisfaction of his conscious mind which all the while has been so little concerned with the debt as to have to look it up to be reminded of it.

This, or something like it, is what the theory of extended telepathy can mean when translated from the language of scientific scepticism into terms of actual behaviour.

Experimental science of course is not primarily concerned with the light relief of this perhaps superficial realism, but with its own close processes of thought based on analytic observation of facts. However, basically abstruse theories must ultimately reflect upon, and be reflected upon, by actuality. Recent thought amongst some psychical researchers draws attention to the lack of direct evidence of extended telepathy between the living, recognising that such theories must themselves be examined as rigorously as positive evidence has to be. As Professor C. A. Mace has pointed out, a

> theory is supported by the failure of its opponents to disprove it. And this is true both of the theories of sceptics as well as the theories of believers. Those who try to prove that telepathy occurs are helped by the attempts (and especially the failures) of those who try to prove that the facts are explained in terms of trickery or subliminal perception ... the same principles

* *Human Personality*, 722B (abbreviated).

of scientific rigour must be applied to attempts to disprove parapsychological hypothesis as are to be applied in attempting to prove such hypotheses.*

Up to now psychical research has largely failed to do this. Such failure throws into high relief the artificial nature of the extended telepathy theory when applied to cases otherwise supporting the survival theory.

2

About thirty years ago psychical research began to take a new turn, and has since concentrated its principal efforts on the laboratory, upon attempts to discover whether telepathy and clairvoyance can be shown to exist by statistical methods. Inevitably there must be a school of researchers who prefer to study material within the precise conditions of the laboratory, and who without laboratory evidence would continue to be unconvinced by spontaneous cases. To them there seems a better hope that the subject matter may be brought here on to firmer ground than could ever be possible in qualitative evidence. For if ESP exists, some of its members have said, it may be possible to observe it at work, in however slight a degree, in ordinary non-mediumistic people under strict conditions, in experiments which can be repeated at will. If this were to come about there would then be virtually no doubt of the existence of telepathy.

Professor Rhine of Duke University, U.S.A., was among the first to carry out systematic experiments devised to enable telepathy to be measured statistically. These are known as quantitative experiments. A Zener pack of twenty-five cards is used, made up of five of each of five different cards, each bearing a simple abstract design; it is obvious therefore that the chance odds of guessing a Zener card correctly are five to one. The early experiments showed overall that a standard was achieved which exceeded chance expectation, but was small numerically. If a sufficiently large number of persons score even such slight successes, the statistical odds that chance would not produce such results are extremely high. The experiments suggested that a number of people have a very dim telepathic faculty.

Rhine discovered one or two star performers who varied very

* Editorial Foreword to *Experimental Psychical Research*, by Dr. R. H. Thouless, p. 12 (Penguin Books).

greatly in their ability from period to period; for a short while, perhaps, their work would include a number of runs astronomically above chance expectation. Once his best worker, Pearce, perceived twenty-five cards correctly out of twenty-five. Then for a period results would drop to chance, or below. Investigation showed that fatigue, worry, pre-occupation, or any slight use of drugs or alcohol tended to banish the telepathic faculty. On the other hand, occasional high scoring of Zener cards has been observed in later years in subjects under hallucinogenic drugs.

In the opinion of some researchers, subsequent statistical experiments have sufficiently often produced negative results to cast some doubts on the findings of Rhine's early tests. Quantitative experiments have reached a very high degree of sophistication in detecting whether or not laboratory ESP exists, and in order to test also whether clairvoyance is at work, machines with elaborate electrical circuits have been devised to eliminate any living mind from knowing which card is being presented to the percipient to guess.

An outstanding set of experiments was carried out by Doctor Soal. These were found to give only chance results, but were then recalculated as if the percipients had tried to guess the next card, and again the next card but one, instead of the card to which they had actually given their attention. It was then found that the new calculations showed results astronomically above chance expectation. Further experiments were therefore made to discover if similar results arose when this prophetic guessing was intended, and this produced extremely strong statistical evidence in favour of precognition.

Doubt has later been raised as to whether, although the statistical method as at present calculated was correctly applied in all these cases, statistical thought may not after all relate itself to randomness correctly.* Statistical evidence of telepathy may possibly turn out in expert opinion not to be valid after all, that is to say in the way it has hitherto been calculated to be. However, orthodox views of statistics must prevail in psychical research at present.

The value of quantitative experiment is that through laboratory techniques it may finally reach a conclusive proof of the *existence* of ESP, of a kind which no amount of spontaneous cases can ever provide, because the latter depend upon human testimony, and not on statistical measurement. On the negative side, the value of this laboratory work

* *Proc. 50, Biology and Psychical Research*, Professor A. C. Hardy, F.R.S., p. 97.

is held to be that if, after repeated testing, the existence of ESP cannot be established, then doubt will thereby fall also on the accuracy of the many observations made in early experiments and in spontaneous cases.

A fundamental weakness of quantitative work, which at first sight is so precise and clear-cut in its approach, is that there are inescapable limitations in laboratory work which may prevent telepathy from functioning there in any strength. It has long been realised that exercise of the ESP faculty does not flourish under laboratory conditions, it wilts. The more complicated the technique becomes, in order that it may be enabled to sift results with ever-increasing fineness, it tends by its very complications to inhibit the percipients so that there becomes little or nothing to sift. There is also some ground for believing that what telepathy best transfers is "not so much an act or cognition, or a piece of information ... but rather a feeling or an emotion."* In short, all experimental percipients, including mediums (who are particularly bad at laboratory work) get bored, and after a while their successes tend to drop. If continued long enough, their total figures, even after including any original high scores, tend to decline nearer and nearer to those of chance expectation, and may finally equal it. Were their original high guesses then due to telepathy or only to chance? The statistical method can possibly dilute and eventually even conceal the existence of genuine laboratory telepathy, if the latter is sporadic. This is a danger of which those using the method are of course very well aware.

In discussing ESP, Professor Richet's analogy is worth remembering: that some natural phenomena, such as meteorites, cannot be produced at will, but they undoubtedly exist.

If quantitative work finally does produce unchallengeable positive results, it needs to be asked how real these are, how much the statistics are able to tell us about the nature of telepathy, apart from measuring its presence. They cannot for instance satisfactorily measure vividness. How far can one truly say that the odds of 10,000 to 1 that chance would not produce similar results are a hundred times more significant than odds of 100 to 1, when it really only represents a few extra cards guessed amongst a much larger number of failures? If it comes to be accepted that quantitative research has established that mankind in general has a rudimentary ESP faculty, it will still of course be neces-

* *Proc.* Vol. 49, p. 163. Presidential Address: Dr. Gilbert Murray.

sary to use other methods to discover what the faculty can do when working more freely in the qualitative field outside the laboratory. In fact one is back to where psychical research largely started, back to qualitative work, to potentially richer quarries which quantitative work can supplement but can never replace. Quantitative work pays for its precision by having to accept severe limitations in the field in which it can operate.

3

Let us turn to the second set of difficulties, internal difficulties which are of quite a different kind from those so far described. Some of them are quite formidable.

(a) The scientific evidence depends on very few mediums. The S.P.R. has good evidence from perhaps half a dozen first-class mediums, professional and amateur, and a handful of automatic writers. Outside the S.P.R. the evidence of many other professional mediums has largely to be set aside for the simple reason that it has almost never been carefully enough recorded. Some minds consider that it would be extremely unwise to accept so important a fact as survival so long as the S.P.R. evidence continues to have been drawn from perhaps one person out of many hundred thousand. This criticism is a weighty objection, which must rightly give many people pause. Nevertheless this criticism is in substance a demand for a larger amount of evidence. It is an objection which time may remove.

(b) The evidence is derived from mediums who, whether in trance or not, are in a rare, highly sensitised and abnormal state of consciousness. Some minds ask that survival, if it be true, should be capable of proof through normal mental conditions and not only through abnormal ones, or if not abnormal at least highly unusual. That it is thus apparently abnormal or unusual makes it liable to the suspicion that mediumship is only a pathological condition, and likely to be productive only of illusory results.

(c) It is often said that no material of intellectual or philosophical value has emerged from mediumistic sources. This objection will be discussed in a later chapter.

(d) In the scientific records, when the soi-disant dead are contacted, it sometimes seems that only a small and uncertain part, a slender thread of the original personality, is available. If these are indeed the full surviving personalities they claim to be, why is it, as is undoubtedly sometimes the case, that the true things they say are embedded in matter which is false or inconsequential, why is it above all that they are at times reduced to so apparently tenuous a grasp even upon the contents of their own memories? Why do they sometimes seem to be unaware of what they have said at a previous sitting, perhaps only a few days earlier? This is a first-class qualitative objection and a very weighty one.

Obviously it may arise because the soi-disant communicators are not really there at all, but only represent a mental artefact of some kind, nourished upon information drawn together by telepathy from the sitter, and possibly by extended telepathy from elsewhere, forming a jumble of assorted memories filched from living minds and worked up by the dramatising subconscious mind of the medium. Alternatively the communicators may be there, but find some block between themselves and the listener. If there is a block, it seems curiously intermittent.

We have to accept the rubbish, the occasional astonishing inaccuracies, which are a disquieting feature of parts of many seances which psychical research has recorded, and which make some communications so spasmodic; at times accurate and purposeful; at others, almost worthless; possibly at the start of a sitting quite meaningless, then running perfectly clear, and then perhaps towards the end trailing off again into inconsequence.

Take for example the G.P. case summarised in Chapter 2 in the words of Dr. Hodgson, the researcher in charge of Mrs. Piper's work. When thus isolated in the report, the evidence is positive, it can even be said to be startling. But it is not the whole story; it has also to be looked at in the light of G.P.'s later utterances after the Hodgson report had been drawn up, and also in the light of Mrs. Piper's work as a whole. For the G.P. communicator declined later on, and what he said some years after often proved to be confused and confusing. This is of course damaging evidence against him. It could be said that G.P. (if indeed it was he) would have done much better had he been satisfied with his earlier efforts, and had left well alone. It can certainly be put forward that by the time of the later appearances he may have lost many of his earth-memories, as in fact another communicator – himself of extremely doubtful authenticity – said of him that he had; but little account can be taken of such a statement by psychical researchers who are engaged in seeking evidence of G.P.'s alleged survival of a still more rigorous kind than had already been given in his early communications.

At this later time another set of controls were appearing in Mrs. Piper's trance, claiming to be the same controls who had operated through another medium, the Rev. Stainton Moses. These controls used the same pseudonyms as through Stainton Moses, but entirely failed, when challenged, to state their alleged true historical names as originally given to him, and which had never been made public; when asked for these names through Mrs. Piper, they gave totally different ones. These new controls often spoke utter nonsense, claiming for instance to have met after their death well-known characters in fiction, such as Adam Bede, as if they had been real persons. Now G.P. in his later confused appearances seems to guarantee these controls.*

It has been said by researchers that this also throws doubt upon the validity of the early powerful evidence of his survival, for if the later G.P. had so little grasp upon his own and others' reality as he apparently had, does not this indicate that the earlier evidence may have had its source in living persons' memories and not as it seemed at the time in the surviving G.P.? The more fragmentary and confused the later G.P. became, the more reasonable it became to suspect that what earlier on purported to come from him was a mere amalgam drawn from living minds.

On the other hand it is hard to be certain that at some stage the original G.P. communicator may not have withdrawn. The later confusions could have arisen from a pseudo-G.P. which had its origin, like Professor Soal's Ferguson, in the mind of sitters who expected further G.P. appearances, or else arose only from a reflection in the medium's mind. Some of the G.P. appearances may have been true, and others wholly false.

Again, we may not be justified in rejecting wholly the possibility that G.P. *was* confused for a while. For a third period arose still later on, when Mrs. Piper's mediumship was producing improved evidence, and G.P. then appeared briefly from time to time, intervening from the background to clear up momentary misunderstandings between communicators and sitters, and during this period he referred to an earlier time when the researchers had got him confused. The evidence leaves room for different valuations of the G.P. personality.

* *Proc.*, Vol. 15, p. 24.

Because in this way evidence sometimes seems to contradict its earlier parts; because it is not consistently sustained; because it can sometimes be studded with inaccuracies about the most central facts of the purporting survivor's earth life – as for instance when a mother apparently fails to state correctly the number of her own children – researchers are reluctant to give to other strikingly accurate parts of the evidence the full weight they would otherwise command. The worst can at times be so bad that it confounds the best, making the latter difficult to believe in. This element of dilution in what would otherwise be strong evidence is an important factor in persuading researchers to hold on for so long to the extended telepathy theory in spite of the weaknesses and difficulties which it possesses.

The series of non-survivalist explanations remains available as an armoury, each item of which can and must be used in the scrutiny of all future evidence.

Some researchers, whilst accepting that no single one of these explanations will fit all the cases, ask whether between them these are sufficient to account for all the purported evidence of survival. This case has been closely argued by Professor E. R. Dodds in a much respected paper "Why I do not believe in Survival".*

As against this, the fact that five or six different explanations are required suggests to some minds that it is unlikely that these, so diverse from one another, will between them neatly and completely dovetail into one another so as to account for all the evidence. The researcher also finds himself then driven to separating the various phenomena instead of bringing them together.

Perhaps the most fundamental difficulty, one which is shared by both the main lines of thought in psychical research – the line which has applied to qualitative evidence the theory of extended telepathy, and the other line which has turned for so long to quantitative experiments in the laboratory – is to be found in what is probably the most characteristic feature in ESP material, its capriciousness and unreliability. In the G.P. case we have an illustration of how it makes its appearance in qualitative evidence. When researchers turned to the laboratory, possibly in some exasperation, in the hope that there ESP might prove capable of stabilisation as well as of quantitive measurement, it was only to find that ESP is in another way as elusive in the laboratory as outside it.

* *Proc.*, Vol. 42.

Scientists have found themselves equally unable to predict when ESP will make an appearance in the laboratory and are quite unable to direct or control its operations; they can do no more than give it an opportunity to appear.

Where have these two lines of thought led? Today it begins to look as though the value of both lines has been no more than reductive and critical; both of course have been a very necessary discipline to which the evidence was bound to be subjected. After many years of close attention, there has resulted a failure to harness telepathy in such a way that it functions sufficiently effectively in the laboratory for more to be learned of its mysteries. It has not proved repeatable in the way scientists like to find an experiment repeatable. In one way it would be more satisfactory to the scientific mind if it never appeared at all in the laboratory, but this did not happen either.

In qualitative work it is ineffective to have to continue to posit the existence of extended telepathy without being able to find how to discover its limits in any way at all and at the same time to lack any real independent evidence of its existence.

Quantitatively, then, there is less decisive evidence than the researcher has hoped to obtain, and qualitatively there is much more than he can satisfactorily account for, and some of this, in the opinion of some researchers, points strongly towards the probability of survival. Psychical research is likely to continue to be largely ineffectual until a sufficient number of researchers can agree to set up some sort of working hypothesis, however imperfect, on the basis of which further investigations can be carried out.

Until then, there will continue to be room within it, as at present, for a great many shades of opinion from the conviction of the strong probability of survival reached by some eminent researchers to the scepticism, complete or all but complete, of others equally eminent. The general verdict of psychical research towards survival so far necessarily remains one of Not Proven.

CHAPTER FOUR

Further Difficulties

I

COMPLEX difficulties lie hidden within what is often acknowledged, that survival is the most simple explanation of the data of psychical research. The survival hypothesis is simple in that it can explain the data and does not require the extravagances of the extended telepathy theory. In that sense only is it simple. It is very far from being simple when we try to understand *how* survival and communication can be. It involves a number of scientific mysteries. Because a thing remains a scientific mystery, it does not mean of course that it does not happen; but it can mean that it is very difficult meanwhile to accept that it happens. At present telepathy between the living remains a mystery, possibly telepathy between the living and the dead is a greater mystery still. We have no scientific understanding of the conditions under which it can be possible for a man to continue existence apart from the body, and in particular apart from the brain, which in life appears to condition him so closely.

The present case against survival is that it is unnecessary, premature, and too simple, to bring everything together under this single hypothesis, especially since some cases of possible communication from the dead, as we have seen, strongly resemble cases which undoubtedly are telepathic communications between the living. The facts admit of survival, but do not enforce it; the researcher must go with the facts, but not an inch further. His task is to take the utmost precautions not to go an inch further. That is why many of them consider it wise not to adopt as yet any working hypothesis.

Observation is only the first part of the scientific process; until the observations of psychical research can be assimilated into the general picture of the universe built up by specialised studies in other scientific fields, they are incomplete, they do not possess a full scientific existence. They have to be explained as well as observed before science as a whole can accept them as established.

The observations themselves seem generally unlikely to scientists, even apart from their implications. New investigators, instead of accepting the work of their predecessors as they would be prepared to do in other scientific studies, often insist upon going back to the start and seeing if they too observe what others have already found. Partly because of this constant going over the old ground, this inability to believe the facts, little advance has been made in grappling with the remarkable evidence contained in *Proceedings*. Both telepathy and survival by implication contradict a number of hypotheses built up by patient scientific observation in other fields over many years which suggest that life is bound to end with the life of the body. The majority of scientists would consider it highly unlikely that these will be upset by the precarious and baffling observations of psychical research. To accept all the implications of survival would require a great deal of scientific re-thinking in these other well-established fields. Orthodox scientific opinion in general so far remains massively unimpressed by psychical research.

To the scientist whose work has not included any first-hand study of it, psychical research possesses a very slender status. As long as it does not advance any coherent working hypothesis of its own, it is clearly not yet strong enough to influence the main body of science. It remains at present a cinderella of sciences, and occupies, although its subject-matter might become so very momentous, only one very small corner in the wide field of scientific attention. It is regarded as a sub-department of abnormal psychology, which in turn is a sub-department of psychology, which is itself considered by many to be only a quasi-science, because a human being in his totality is a subject impossible to study with scientific exactitude. Psychical research is a minnow, swimming alongside the giant whales of biology and physics. Its evidence will have to become very strong and decisive if it is to influence these main streams of scientific thought. When it is in conflict with these, scientists will in general prefer the deductions drawn from these broad and well-confirmed fields, rather than the observations of psychical research derived only from a small, marginal and abnormal field.

The researcher himself is immensely handicapped in that in all the most central part of the material it is only possible to observe its results, and not the processes by which these results are obtained. These are screened from him because he cannot see and hear as a medium claims to be able to do. To him the medium's observations are alien and suspect. It is a little as if a doctor, called on to decide the state of a patient's health, is not allowed to hear the patient's story, but has to rely only upon what a witch-doctor tells him about it. So the researcher's distrust of mediumistic practices because he cannot carry them out for himself adds to his hesitation before the already difficult facts which confront him.

There is another reason why, in the matter of survival, scientists are likely to feel an especial reluctance to set up a hypothesis based on probability until the facts have been seen for a long time to be a good deal stronger than would be required before setting up working hypotheses in other fields. For, if and when such a hypothesis is produced, scientists know that the lay mind is likely to turn a probability at once into a certainty, and to fly to irrational assumptions based on survival, for which it will immediately claim scientific sanction. Science cannot prevent such a thing happening, but it goes very much against the scientific sense of responsibility to encourage it at all. So there is a scientific conscience with great integrity behind it which is doubly cautious against any premature setting-up of a working hypothesis of survival. Natural scientific caution increases also in this field of evidence of survival, because of the very importance of the human implications involved. Whatever direction these eventually lead towards, they are bound to be pregnant with philosophical meaning and ethical overtones. Nevertheless, since a probability is an acceptable basis for a working hypothesis in other scientific fields, ultimately, provided the facts are considered to justify it, it will doubtless also prove acceptable in this.

2

Research has its necessary limitations which are determined by its proper methods; indeed it is valid precisely because it insists on these limitations. However it cannot be overlooked that limitations of another kind can creep in from time to time, without in any way invalidating its proper approach. Although the S.P.R. holds no collective opinion, it comes like any other body of people to have a dominant temper which rules it, and which undergoes changes from time to time. Some recent tendencies in psychical research can be regarded as little more than exercises in scepticism.

Inevitably there will gravitate towards the S.P.R. a certain number of negative, compulsive, or professional sceptics. A negative sceptic might be said to be one who sits on the fence for pleasure as much as from necessity. He prefers contradicting others' facts to making direct observations of his own, and his work is largely confined to what Professor Wilson Knight has tartly called studying other people's studies. The Society is something of a natural home for these, and indeed there is a legitimate work for them to do; the Society would be the poorer without them. A favourite method of the negative sceptic is to examine evidence which is many years old, and was observed by somebody else. He then invents some possible alternative explanation, and looks around for supporting facts which *might* have been present. He does not produce any direct evidence to show that this alternative really took place. It remains speculation and is unprovable. However, it cannot be shown that it could not have happened, so the sceptic claims that the factual evidence, the product of direct observation on the part of his predecessor, is unreliable. The sceptic is justified when he can point out where a previous observer's precautions were not stringent enough, and can show where there is need for further precautions in new experiments. The work of the negative sceptic is corrective, not creative. A line has to be drawn between productive scepticism, and an attitude which has the intention of preventing any positive hypothesis from ever being advanced.

It is now being put forward, as we have seen, that negative hypotheses should be considered as unacceptable unless supported by as much evidence as is required of a positive hypothesis, and this surely is a healthy trend in psychical research.

Amongst psychical researchers there are progressives and reactionaries as there are everywhere else, and from time to time the balance in the S.P.R. falls differently between them. However different in individual opinion, psychical research has never been without workers of massive scientific integrity.

Psychical research tells the truth it finds, but because of its framework of entirely necessary and honourable limitations, it can tell only part of the truth. This is of course recognised and accepted by psychical researchers. The part of the truth it can tell may in the end turn out to be a great deal less than the whole; that will depend upon the value of what falls outside its ken. In asking whether the approach of psychical research is more reliable, more true and more important than other approaches, it must not be forgotten that this is something which by its own terms of reference, psychical research cannot itself estimate. It can only estimate whether it is carrying out its own proper tasks as well as possible. It may in time produce reasons of its own which operate strongly for or against survival, but it can never itself assess the reasons of a quite different kind for or against survival, which appeal to man's other faculties, for these require judgments which are other than of a scientific kind.

CHAPTER FIVE

Test Cases

I

BUT, surely, it may be said, the root of the matter – as distinct from the complicated explorations which may afterwards be needed to understand and explain it – can be settled by a few simple and decisive test-cases or even by one master case? The G.P. case, the Pearl Tie-pin and Shark cases are all strong cases – the R.101 case, which is one of the strongest cases outside psychical research, is described in Chapter 10 – but the fact remains, whatever the reasons for it, that these cases have not satisfied all psychical researchers. Why should not one indisputable incontrovertible case of survival be produced, a test case which will settle the issue once and for all? This too is a very difficult problem. It has engaged the attention of researchers over many years. Sir Oliver Lodge once contributed a paper to the S.P.R. in which he tried to devise the evidence which Betsy Trotwood would need to produce in order to prove her survival, but it appeared that whatever she might be imagined to say through a medium, her evidence would not lead to more than a *probability* of her survival. It will be found to be very hard indeed, in fact impossible, to devise even an imaginary test-case which is absolutely water-tight, and which will not in some way rest upon probability, however strong in degree.

Let us cite a simple unsophisticated case of a test.

The Finney Test

Rockland, Mass. April 19, 1891.

Mr. Hodgson,
DEAR SIR,

Some weeks ago I received from you a few lines asking me to give you an account of the communication received from Benja in spirit-life, some twenty-five years ago.

For weeks and months before my brother left the form we conversed freely on the subject of spirit communion and such matters, and one morning he requested me to bring him a small piece of brick, also pen and ink; he then made two marks on one side, and one on the other with the ink, then breaking the brick in two, gave me one piece, telling me at the time to take care of it, and someday he would hide the other piece away where no one but himself would know, and after leaving the form, if possible, would return in some way and tell me where it was. I could then compare together, and it would be a test that he could return and communicate . . . After he left the form . . . for months we got nothing satisfactory.

We then commenced sitting at the table at home (mother and myself) which we did for some little time; at last it commenced tipping, and by calling the alphabet spelled out where we could find the piece of brick that he put away . . . By calling the alphabet we spelled out – "You will find that piece of brick in the cabinet under the tomahawk. Benja."

I went to that room and took the key, unlocked the cabinet, which had not been touched by any one after he locked it and put away the key. There I found that piece of brick just as it had spelled out, and it corresponded with the piece I had retained, fitting on exactly where he broke it off the piece I had. It was wrapped in a bit of paper and tucked into a shell, and placed in the bottom of the cabinet *exactly under* the tomahawk, as was spelled out . . . The piece of brick was entirely concealed in the shell, so that it could not be seen from outside the cabinet. It was wrapped in a piece of paper stuck together with mucilage and tucked into the end of the shell, then a piece of paper gummed over that, so that nothing was visible from the shell. The shell was on the lower shelf of the cabinet, and only the top of the shell was visible outside the cabinet.

One more little incident I will mention . . . He wrote me a letter (about the time he gave me the piece of brick) and sealed it, saying at the time it was not to be answered, but the contents of the letter to be told. I got that in the same way I did the other, by calling the alphabet and the table tipping. It was these words – "Julia! do right and be happy – Benja". That was correct. Just the contents of my letter . . .

JULIA A. FINNEY[*]

The brick and shell were sent to the investigator, Dr. Hodgson, but not the letter.

Now Mrs. Finney's honesty has not been doubted, but the case rests upon her unsupported word, and she was the sole surviving member of her family when she described the test, which had taken place twenty-five years previously. A case which is to be made into a finally decisive one, or rather one which is intended to be such, would essentially need to be contemporaneously observed, and observed very strictly, by experienced psychical researchers.

Myers suggested that everyone should attempt such a test as the Finney one, and if success resulted, presumptive evidence of survival

[*] *Human Personality*, 876.

would be gradually built up. This would be strong, cumulative evidence, but if each case were isolated from the others, some theoretical weakness, however slender, would almost certainly be found in every one. The best person to devise a test case ought to be a psychical researcher.

2

Where lies the essential difficulty inherent in any deliberately devised test case? It lies here: if the proof is to be confirmed, this confirmation must already exist, either in writing, or else residing in the knowledge or memories of some living person. Therefore it can always be held to have been discovered by a medium from this source, instead of from the dead person. Suppose that this record is in writing, and that it is never communicated to anybody, but is concealed in opaque coverings, and then deposited with the S.P.R. or at a bank. We have still not devised a satisfactory technique, for what is recorded in writing can be conceived to be discoverable through clairvoyance, even through distant clairvoyance. If the test has to be confirmed through the memories of a living person, it is from here that the information may be deemed to have been discovered, after the death of the person making the test, by the medium or percipient. Again, since the dead person doubtless devised his test with care, it is possible that, in so doing, he left, whilst alive, a strong latent telepathic impression which, after his death, might in some way be recovered and picked up by the medium. However unlikely these explanations may sometimes be, they make it impossible for these tests to be considered water-tight. This problem has never been fully solved – how to devise a formal test which can be satisfied posthumously with absolute certainty and without access to the solution being theoretically available to the medium.

Myers himself made a test, and so did Oliver Lodge. The Myers test was a failure. Mrs. Verrall, the wife of a Cambridge don and herself a Newnham lecturer, and an automatic writer for the S.P.R., felt she had produced in her script the contents of the sealed letter which Myers had left; on opening the letter, this proved to be totally incorrect.*

---

* In Proc. Vol. 52, p.187, more recently available evidence is adduced to suggest that the Myers test may after all have been partially successful. But there is quite certainly nothing conclusive about it.

Sir Oliver Lodge made it known that his test was concerned with some fact about himself which he had never told to a living soul. Cautiously he added that he would be in no hurry to transmit it after his death. The test was a complicated one; he deposited eleven envelopes with the S.P.R. and five with the London Spiritualist Alliance.* The Myers envelope had depended upon a single trial; once his envelope had been opened, the test could never be attempted again. The heart of Lodge's message was contained in two identical envelopes, one at the S.P.R. and one at the L.S.A.; these would be opened last of all. The contents of the earlier envelopes were to perform a double task; that of giving preliminary hints which might stimulate the memory of the posthumous Lodge if this should prove sluggish, and that of helping to eliminate faulty early messages which might be erroneously claimed as coming from him. At later stages of the experiment some of these hints were made known to sitters and mediums. No medium was able to produce a clear-cut account of what the final envelopes, when opened, were found to describe – a lifelong habit of Lodge's of drumming his fingers in a certain way to follow a musical tune. The best attempt was made by Jordan Gill, a well-known professional medium, and suggested a degree of partial and imperfect apprehension of the contents. As a test, it certainly failed. Its method was criticised by researchers on the grounds that it would be likely to result in attempts which would prove incomplete and would allow room for differences in judgment as to their degree of accuracy, as proved to be the case. The test did not overcome the difficulty that the contents of the final envelopes might be read clairvoyantly. It was also thought that the hints in the earlier envelopes might eventually enable the substance of the final message to be partly guessed, or even rationally inferred.

As a result of these weaknesses, Doctor Thouless has endeavoured to improve upon the Lodge test, and has devised a different kind of test, one which endeavours with great virtuosity to overcome the difficulties hitherto encountered. The test consists of two coded messages, one in which the code is theoretically unbreakable, and the other in which though theoretically breakable the code is considered by experts to be extremely unlikely to be broken.

When Doctor Thouless dies, he will be called upon, in order to demonstrate his survival, to give through a medium two words which

* Now known as the College of Psychic Science.

are the key to one cipher, and a continuous passage which will be the key to the second one.

The great advantage of the test – and here lies the brilliance of its design – is that the coded message is meanwhile available during his lifetime to any cipher expert, as well as to any medium who likes to try to discover the keys by telepathically extracting them from Dr. Thouless's mind before he dies. An earlier coded message which Dr. Thouless had made was broken by a cipher expert, hence a more complicated coding system has been used for the two current tests. No medium who has been invited to discover the message from Dr. Thouless's mind has yet succeeded in doing so. There is therefore an increased degree of probability, if success comes only after his death, that Dr. Thouless will then himself have communicated the keys to the medium. The final great advantage of the test is that any number of false attempts can be made without destroying its value for future use.

Even if Dr. Thouless does posthumously give the keys to his ciphers, however, thus considerably increasing the probability of his having survived, it would be very surprising if there proved to be no researchers who would not prefer to attribute the success to latent telepathy, or to whatever alternative explanation they could devise. No success in any test is likely to be wholly safe against the ingenuities of sceptical reasoning.

The early researchers were pioneers in a subject to which scientific attention had never been given before. As time passed on, it came to be seen that there would arise a new aspect in the situation, making possible another sort of test. For what would happen when the first generation of psychical researchers themselves came to die; would there come about sound evidence of *their* survival? Having known from first-hand experience whilst alive the formidable difficulties of gaining conclusive evidence of survival, would they do better, would evidence now come about which would show, or appear to show, posthumous appreciation of the particular difficulties? Would there come about not only personal evidence of themselves, but technically interesting evidence of some new kind, which would attempt to overcome those very difficulties debated by them formerly? Would they be able to overcome, at least in part, the internal difficulties in the case for survival?

When F. W. H. Myers died psychical researchers set about devising a new kind of test, one of a more diffused type, to find out whether a highly-educated classical scholar, as Myers had been, could gradually prove through the little-educated medium Mrs. Piper that he still retained his classical knowledge.

Tests were therefore devised to see if the posthumous Myers could show through Mrs. Piper a knowledge of Latin and Greek, neither of which she knew. A Latin message was read asking him to develop evidence by a new method, which some thought had already commenced in automatic scripts purporting to come from him, a method which was later on to become known as cross-correspondence. The test makes it doubtful if the purported Myers correctly apprehended the meaning. On the other hand, the kind of cross-correspondence requested did appear in considerable number. On another occasion the Lord's Prayer was read in Greek to the purported Myers; it appeared that he did not understand it. When asked which was his favourite Horace Ode, he gave an unexpected answer, which some think characteristic, some not. Asked some simple questions about the Aeneid, Myers did, in time, and with a certain amount of confusion, offer information showing considerable knowledge of the book, and some familiarity with its language, and he made points, and insisted upon them, which were correct but contrary to his questioner's own memory. At another time a translation of the Invocation to Zeus was read, and the posthumous Myers recognised that it came from the Agamemnon, and eventually correctly stated it was by Aeschylus, and formed part of a trilogy.* Again, he was questioned about Lethe, and gave replies which showed more classical knowledge than his questioner possessed, making references to a story in Ovid's Metamorphoses which were not fully recognised until some considerable time after. The book had been a favourite one of the living Myers.

Some words from Plotinus with which he had been familiar were read, and he was asked to translate the Greek, and to say what the quotation suggested to him. He did so indirectly by a highly complex answer, involving reference to a page of his own book, *Human Personality*, and oblique references to his own favourite literary tastes. It also revealed a knowledge of the meaning of the Greek, and it referred to a passage in *In Memoriam* where the Plotinus quotation is indirectly paraphrased.†

The result of these tests is generally accepted as a failure in the Latin message and in the Lord's Prayer test, as inconclusive in the Horace Ode, and as successful in the Plotinus case and in parts of the other

* *Proc.* Vol. 24, pp. 39-85. † *Proc.* Vol. 22, pp. 107-172.

classical cases. The net result is not enough to count as clear-cut evidence that the purported Myers, when operating through Mrs. Piper, knew what the living Myers knew of the classics, even though at times it suggests that he did. Researchers do not eliminate the possibility that the information may somehow have been obtained telepathically from the minds of living scholars, even if some of these had not necessarily been in touch with the medium at any time. It is extremely hard to see how the Myers figure, if he could succeed in a difficult case, could fail very palpably in an easy one. On the other hand, it is equally hard to separate out what may be due, not to gaps in the soi-disant Myers personality, but to defects in the ability of Mrs. Piper's mediumship to record it.

3

But there are strong signs of the posthumous Myers doing something better than trying to answer to the tests of his former colleagues; of his himself initiating and offering evidence of a new type of his own. At about the time of these tests, evidence did begin to reach the S.P.R. which some think points to a widely varied and long sustained attempt over many years on the part of Myers, through a number of different mediums, to prove his survival in his own way, or perhaps it would be better to say in such ways as he found possible. This purported Myers chooses a lady in India, gives to her through her own automatic writing the name and address in Cambridge of a lady whom she had never met, but who turns out to be a classical scholar and amateur S.P.R. medium, Mrs. Verrall, to whom at the same period the posthumous Myers had been giving messages. He describes Mrs. Verrall's husband, speaks of a new evening frock Mrs. Verrall had just bought, and gradually, amongst a lot of mixed and rubbishy material, succeeds in working in references to a number of his favourite classical authors and passages, thus apparently endeavouring to prove the continuity of his mind, its taste and its memory contents.

What is new in this attempt is the complexity of the material given, and the number of mediums used, as contrasted with the simple straightforward evidence of G.P. It is rather as if the posthumous Myers figure leaves largely on one side the facts of his earth-life, and instead attempts to say: "This is what I still am in my mind now." It seems a significant change of emphasis.

During the dozen or so years following Myers's death a new and very subtle method of giving evidence developed; this is by the cross-correspondences referred to in the Latin message.

4

By cross-correspondence is meant an apparent attempt to give a fragment of a message, usually through automatic writing, to one medium, another fragment of the same message through a second, and perhaps another part again through a third, of such a kind that the whole will only be fully understood when the fragments are pieced together.

If one automatist writes "death", a second "mors", and a third "thanatos", it suggests that one mind is at work through all three; in a true cross-correspondence something more is produced than simple repetition of the same idea in different forms: the common factor which solves the puzzle is only introduced at the end, and shows the intended but hitherto unguessed connection between earlier writings through different automatists.

In one type of case, quotations from English and Classical poetry, and fragmentary references which would be understood by educated minds, appear over and over in the writings of several mediums in such a way as to be clearly associated with one another, and to form a motif or theme; ultimately they are found to be a kind of symbolic portrait of a particular dead person, in which the name and some of the events of the life are indicated, thus pointing to a common meaning and purpose concealed from the mediums until a late stage. Thus, in the "Palm Sunday" case, the Hon. Mary Catherine Lyttelton, Lord Balfour's love, who died at the age of 24, was referred to in communications over the years as the palm maiden, a lily, Berenice, the Blessed Damozel, the blossom of the may, as walking with a candle in one hand; the scripts write also of a flaming wheel, maidenhair, patines, and cockleshells; all these conceal references to her names, her family crest, her early death, to a particular photograph, and to her hair which was cut off after her death and preserved in a box.

One of the Verrall scripts appears to explain the intended method in cross-correspondences:

> The quotations are a framework – from the known to the unknown. The gradual emergency of a train of thought can be traced through emphasis

and re-iteration – no, by emphasis and elimination ... I do not think the idea contained in the references to elimination has been clearly grasped. The gradual emergence of a train of thought was spoken of before. Exegesis is an example. The metaphor of the grain – winnowing the chaff.*

When the literature of cross-correspondences is read as a whole, it contains much evidence of an intention to try and show that fragments obtained by different mediums emanated from one common source – the mind of the posthumous Myers, or, later on, the minds also of certain other recently deceased classical scholars. Some of these later cross-correspondences became very elaborate indeed; the Statius and the Ear of Dionysius cases, for instance, are based on very recondite items of scholarly knowledge.

Cross-correspondences are so complex, and are mixed sometimes with so much pointless material that one school of sceptics prefers to believe that any meaning they have was not woven into the message at all by whatever intelligence, living or dead, produced the message, but was merely interpreted into them afterwards by researchers themselves. To others the scripts seem far too pointed and above all too conscious to be dismissed in this way. Each student of the scripts must decide for himself. It cannot be overlooked that the posthumous Myers speaks in some scripts of references he has already given, or hopes he has given, in the scripts of different mediums, so that the scripts themselves imply conscious knowledge of the method.

5

When the soi-disant Myers seems to attempt to say "I am not the mind of the medium, because I show I can stand aside and impart a fragment of my thought to Medium A, another to Medium B, and a third to Medium C, without any of them knowing the work of the others", the psychical researcher replies by saying "You may have shown you can work independently, but you may, on the other hand, still be only the mind of a living person doing unconsciously, or with intent to deceive, just what you claim as a dead person to be doing consciously." In other words, our old friend, extended telepathy, is held to be back at work again. Some living subliminal mind – the most likely is held to be that of the scrupulously honest classical scholar, Mrs. Verrall – is conceived as working through herself, and through

* *Proc.* Vol. 52, p. 185, quoting Helen Verrall Script 267 of June 10th, 1912.

other mediums too, in order to produce false evidence to deceive her own conscious mind by acting exactly as Myers might do if he were trying to prove his own survival.

The purported Myers, in producing cross-correspondences, has still not shot his bolt. We find his influence again in a fascinating series of scripts in which through another amateur S.P.R. medium, Mrs. Willett, the attempt is made to demonstrate and explain the *process* of mediumship and some of the difficulties experienced by these comminicators in managing a medium. In these experiments, another dead researcher, Edmund Gurney, friend of Myers and his colleague in psychical research, purports to take an active part. Quotations from some of the simpler Willett scripts appear in Chapter 9.

Later, some twenty-five years after his death, Myers appears again, and this time produces, with the help of an automatic writer, Geraldine Cummins, a script giving an account of the worlds beyond death. He also speaks soon after to Sir Oliver Lodge through the control of a different medium, Mrs. Leonard, and gives a somewhat guarded approval to the script.

Psychical research calls on us to suppose therefore that if all this activity, which it is interesting to note is so very literary in flavour, which was carried out in his name, did not emanate from Myers, the poet and researcher, it must be put down to a persistent and long-continued attempt to deceive on the part of the subliminal minds of living mediums – it cannot all be put down to Mrs. Verrall, as some researchers were first inclined to suggest, for the activity continued after her death – or alternatively it must be put down to some other permanently anonymous living subliminal mind which psychical research has never been able to name, and which in scripts appearing over many years has had the surprising discipline to carry on this calculated deceit without ever revealing or hinting at its own identity.

At least it can be said that following upon the death of pioneer psychical researchers the evidence took on a new subtlety, whether or not it derives it from them. In the Myers evidence we have something nearer to a portrait in the round than anywhere else in psychical research. The persistence of the Myers figure over so many years and the apparent attempt to give evidence of his survival in ways which indicate a lively interest in psychical research, coupled with an attempt to defeat the problems he had encountered whilst alive, are, when considered as a whole, extremely hard to explain away in terms of extended telepathy. Advocates of extended telepathy, let it be said frankly, can use the theory to little effect when confronted in cross-correspondences with evidence seemingly so clearly initiated by the same mind through several mediums. As the posthumous Myers once asked a living researcher:

> ... Ask what has been the success of Piddington's last experiment? ... But even if the source is human, who carries the thoughts to the receivers? Ask him that.*

And later, with even more emphasis,

> Write the word Selection. Who selects, my friend Piddington? I address this question to Piddington. Who Selects?†

Certainly it gradually became necessary either for the subliminal telepathy theory to be stretched a good deal further even than before, or alternatively the survival of the researchers regarded as strongly probable. "I hope", says the posthumous Myers, "we have succeeded in dethroning to some extent ... that eternal subliminal self."‡

* *Proc.*, Vol. 24, p. 251.
† *Proc.*, Vol. 25, p. 217.
‡ *Proc.*, Vol. 43, p. 286.

CHAPTER SIX

Subjective Factors in Research

I

BECAUSE psychical researchers as such can only evaluate the scientific part of the evidence, the inference must be resisted that what they thus rightly reject by their own standards is therefore of less value, or of no value at all. The point is that its value is of a different kind.

> ... Psychical research has to do with personal experience carried into an impersonal region ... People have a right to their personal experience and their personal opinion on it. Scientific method, while it helps to clarify opinion, may seem to discredit its personal quality. This is not really so. Science separates out and leaves aside the personal and private elements in an experience without denying anything of their reality for the individuals concerned, simple because its business is with public reality. The question is how much of an experience can be set out so as to make it common property. Science turns the communicable part of private experience into social experience, and makes its account of that experience as reliable as possible.*

To this a qualification is needed. It is not quite true to say that it is *the* communicable part of private experience which science turns into social experience; it would be truer to say that it is *a* part, that part which is communicable within a scientific field of reference. Parts of private experience which must be excluded from this field can still be communicated in other ways, and so contribute to a different section of social experience. Some of the private part of an experience can be communicated through the sensibility which enables us to share with one another, however partially, our inner worlds of experience.

It is one thing to say that science does not accept certain evidence because it is not true, but an entirely different thing to say that it does not accept it because it lies in a region where science cannot make a judgment.

This region we must now investigate, and leave aside the very

* *Evidence of Identity* (Kenneth Richmond), p. 107.

cautious viewpoints adopted by psychical researchers and by scientists in general towards the possibility of survival, and begin to consider these other values found through the individual human approach. First it can be seen that these operate at times in a perfectly proper way in psychical researchers themselves.

2

Professor Richet and Sir Oliver Lodge were for many years personal friends and professional colleagues in psychical research. To Richet, survival seemed an impossible hypothesis since it was in complete contradiction to the field of evidence known to him as a physiologist. He consistently thought that in the extra-sensory field the evidence was impossible and absurd, but that it happened. He constantly saw it happen. As to survival, he says:

> I find myself unable to adopt it. Nevertheless I oppose it half-heartedly, for I am quite unable to bring forward any wholly satisfactory counter-theory.

Although the extra-sensory facts observed by Richet failed to fit in with the facts of physiology as he had found these to be during a lifetime of study, this did not prevent him from acknowledging them as facts, though unexplained facts. There was another factor in the background; in the first world war he had lost a dearly loved son, and was almost morbidly anxious not to attempt any personal communication, in order to ensure that his emotions did not upset the purity of his scientific observation. For Richet, the current was entirely set against survival both because of his physiological training and because of his background beliefs. To Lodge, neither of these difficulties existed. To Lodge, the physicist, survival was not an inharmonious concept, and certainly not ridiculous as it seemed to Richet. On the personal side, what appealed to him in religion and poetry also seemed to him harmonious to the idea of survival. Eventually he came to consider that the evidence called for a working hypothesis of survival. It is important to note that the evidence from his son Raymond, as we know from Lodge's work, did not create this attitude, it fulfilled it when he had already reached it after spending many years in studying other people's evidence. Putting Richet and Lodge beside one another, studying as they did with equal scientific integrity much the same records over the years, we see strikingly illustrated, first, the effect of other fields of scientific knowledge upon the approach of different scientists to psychical research, and second, the effect of their private philosophical backgrounds. However soundly based on solid observation each worker was, however they shared agreement in a common field of observational facts, it cannot fail to be seen that there is an element of private judgment involved in their differing interpretations of these common facts.

3

Now in addition to this subjective colouring of the interpretive judgment, influenced by the scientific and psychological background of the researcher, there is of course a second and quite different subjective factor, of the kind already discussed. The first lies in the mind of the individual scientist and contributes to the total field of scientific opinion within which the facts are discussed and interpreted; the second lies in the material itself. This, as was said in Chapter 1, calls for a sensing of the reality or otherwise of the alleged presence of a communicator who had been known in life to the investigator; what Lodge faced in his own Raymond evidence as distinct from his earlier tests where he was concerned with evidence which could be assessed by him as a third person. It is this extra factor which makes personal communication an experience as well as an assessment. This element is well recognised by psychical research. Because it is not susceptible of exact measurement, it cannot be brought fully into the scientific picture, and yet it forms much of the material which scientific judgment has to sift in order to select the factors it can use.

A few researchers, it is true, have tried to devise for it a method of objective assessment, but inevitably without success. It is a mistaken approach to attempt to measure where precise measurement can never be. The Birge-Pratt attempt to give a statistical rating to these qualitative assessments is a completely unconvincing document. It is a very real difficulty; scientific method cannot, as such, deal with all the material in psychical research. The heart of much of the best material has, in addition to and closely interwoven with its objective facts, a basically subjective aspect which calls for a subjective assessment from the person most closely concerned. A deep wedge of subjectivity cuts into the orderly line of objective scientific scrutiny. This is undoubtedly one reason why many scientists fight shy of psychical research altogether. There is a constant embarrassment to scientists in this saturation of the material with subjective elements, which it is impossible wholly to isolate.

This wedge has to be dealt with by something other than objective judgment. The difficulty is sometimes met by excluding material on the undoubtedly true ground that obligations of privacy, or preferences in the direction of personal reticence demand it. The Rt. Hon. Gerald Balfour, for instance, states how great was the value *to him* of the parts suppressed in the Willett scripts. "It would be impossible to do justice to the argument in favour of spirit communication on the basis of the Willett phenomena without violating confidences which I am bound to respect."*

Scientific enquiry finds, then, that the evidence leads gradually from facts which can be accurately counted and checked to a further element which passes beyond the compass of scientific process; this is one inherent difficulty in demanding scientific proof and scientific proof alone. The section of facts in the field of evidence which can be scientifically checked is only a part of the whole material, and, from one point of view, an impoverished part; as soon as it becomes emotionally enriched it passes beyond the possibility of strict measurement.

Within the facts given by a medium as evidence of survival – names, occupations, relatives, interests, anecdotes and the like – lies a distinction between two sorts of facts; bald facts which have no significance beyond their immediate content, which, one might say, end with themselves and are simply correct or incorrect; and another sort of facts which bear emotional significance which may be detected only by the recipient, which indeed can even have an unspoken element, which thins out into nothingness as soon as a researcher assesses it strictly, as he must. Is the recipient never to accept an unspoken inference, even when it seems clear to him that the words actually spoken were said with just that purpose in mind?

How can this arise? Suppose for instance a purporting communicator says to her husband, "When I was a girl, I lived in a house with a rose garden"; this is a fact which ends with itself, and even though correct, is by no means a distinctive piece of evidence. If however she said "Do you remember the house with the rose-garden?" the phrasing at least suggests something more meaningful; suppose it to be the case

* *Proc.*, Vol. 43, p. 45.

that it was in such a rose garden that the husband proposed marriage to his wife? When, if ever, is he entitled to suppose that the communicator was reminding him of common memories? When is he entitled to complete from his own memory what he believes to be her intended statement? If this was her meaning, why then, one must ask, did she not say so? Unfortunately the alleged communicator often does not say so, does not cross the t's and dot the i's, and perhaps after all cannot be expected always to take cognisance of the niceties of psychical research. Again, she may not be able to say so because she cannot get the medium to reproduce all that she wants to impart. Now suppose there is a whole group of such inferential statements; it is difficult for a researcher to accept that a cumulative effect arises, because it disappears when each statement is taken, as he has to take it, one by one. This is one reason why a piece of evidence often seems so much stronger to the survivalist, who accepts this factor in it, than to a researcher who does not. Which is the truer meaning to be attached to the evidence – its cumulative meaning, or its isolated facts? To a researcher it has to be the latter; to record the material properly for his requirements involves a certain unavoidable impoverishment of it.

There can be another element in the sitting, a vocal factor, which the researcher can do his best to describe, but which depends upon subjective assessment. We have to rely upon this assessment of how vivid, how vraisemblant it is. In a script, even, there can be a quasi-vocal element. The Statius cross-correspondence scripts, which are claimed to emanate from the mind of the deceased scholar Dr. Verrall, are thus described by his intimate friend the Rev. M. A. Bayfield:

> All this is Verrall's manner to the life in animated conversation... When I first read the words... I received a series of little shocks, for the turns of speech are Verrall's, the high-pitched emphasis is his, and I could hear the very tones in which he would have spoken each sentence... We have here an extraordinarily faithful representation of Verrall in respect of a peculiar kind of impatience and a habit of emphasis which he had in conversation, and of his playfulness and sense of humour. In what way are these lifelike touches of character introduced? How are they worked into the essential matter of the scripts? Have they the air of being inserted by an ingenious forger (the unprincipled subliminal of some living person) with a purpose... or do they give us the impression of being spontaneous and genuine? Unless I am inexcusably mistaken, no one accustomed to estimate the internal evidence afforded by a document of doubtful origin could hesitate as to the answer... To me, at least, it is incredible that even the cleverest could

achieve such an unexampled triumph in deceptive impersonation as this would be if the actor is not Verrall himself.*

4

One of the most skilled, cautious and persistent of researchers was Mrs. Sidgwick, whose work for the S.P.R. stretched over fifty years. Her husband, Professor Henry Sidgwick, was one of the founders of the S.P.R.; she herself was Principal of Newnham College for many years. A paper read to the S.P.R. in 1932 by her brother, the Rt. Hon. Gerald Balfour, on her election as President of Honour after so many years' work in the Society, set forth an important distinction. It said: "Conclusive proof of survival is notoriously difficult to obtain. But the evidence may be such as to produce *belief*, even though it falls short of conclusive proof. I have Mrs. Sidgwick's assurance . . . that, upon the evidence before her, she herself is a firm believer both in survival and in the reality of communication." As Tyrrell remarked, "Many will disagree; but none are likely to be in a better position to form a valid judgment so far as the present evidence is concerned."†

Some psychical researchers, like Lodge, have judged that the evidence is strong enough to call for a working hypothesis of survival. Others, like Mrs. Sidgwick, although holding it not scientifically proved, have come to believe in survival on the grounds of what seems to them to be a valid subjective assessment. Mrs. Sidgwick's belief was something other than scientific conviction, though to her there was an element of harmony between the two. Certainly it had been very slowly and hardly won.

At some stage or other the present-day researcher has to ask himself whether or not he is going to decide to give freedom to the rest of his nature, that which is other than his scientific side, to scrutinise, by the light of its own different values, the evidence available in the scientific records, and also to seek to enrich it by his own personal evidence. The researcher has every right to decide that whilst actually engaged in research he will try to concern himself only with what can be made completely scientifically objective. One must respect the invincible repugnance which some scientists feel towards bringing together the

* *Proc.*, Vol. 37, pp. 244–9. See also *Evidence of Personal Survival from Cross Correspondences* (H. F. Saltmarsh), pp. 141–2.
† *The Personality of Man* (G. N. M. Tyrrell), p. 167.

scientific and non-scientific aspects of their mind. But to another type of scientist, to ignore altogether other elements which he knows to exist in the material he is studying, because they can only be considered with another part of his nature than the scientific part, would be to act otherwise than as an integrated human being.

Direct experience enters into and interweaves itself with research; the two cannot be wholly separated. The evidence is constantly tending to take the investigator into realms where he has to think in other ways than as a scientist.

It is just such private experience which, interwoven into her psychical research, created a slowly growing conviction of a personal kind in Mrs. Sidgwick. It resulted in an inward assent which gradually brought itself about in the non-scientific part of her nature, and which she did not feel to be out of harmony with the facts scientifically observed.

The spiritualistic evidence, when the rubbish sometimes associated with its presentation is stripped away, is largely based on private experience. Each person in turn, once he decides to step beyond the necessary limitations of science, depends upon his own personal qualities. Very few have Mrs. Sidgwick's formidable powers of cool, cautious assessment. The act of assessing one's own experiences is fraught with danger, the danger of one's own weaknesses – but then so is every positive action in life. Between oneself and the recognition of a communicator lies a smoke-screen, made up of one's suggestibility, one's faults of observation and of judgment, and one's will-to-believe or, equally, one's will-to-disbelieve. In time perhaps we come to make a subjective value-judgment that we have received a true communication from the dead. It is no more scientific than when we judge a business adviser to be honest or a scoundrel, or than when we accept and believe in the rectitude of our friends, or at least in the rectitude of their relationship to us. The tests and checks we care to make are of a different character than are made in scientific work. Our subjective test of the probability of survival begins in the strength or otherwise of our own power to recognise in a communicator the surviving personality of someone we have known very well. Since, as we have seen, this is partly a private, non-communicable experience, it is to that degree scientifically inadmissible. A psychical researcher would name its acceptance as personal conviction short of, and below, proof; to the recipient, it is an experience which lies in a different field from the problems of scientific proof, and a far more vivid one. We may come so to value that experience that it influences our view of the nature of our eventual future and we decide to live out our life accordingly. We make a value judgment. We are now very far away indeed from scientific proof. We are concerned with an experience of which we have to ask whether it is possible for it to become woven into the very fabric of consciousness, and change it. Such an experience is not easily won; it demands a price, certainly a heavier price than many Spiritualists ever consider paying for it.

5

If a valid personal conviction of survival can be won outside science, why trouble with the difficulties of scientific proof at all? Clearly that would be a very limited position to take up. Science has its own validity, to which many choose to give their allegiance; they look for their sanction there and not from within; in some fields they will not tread within the hazards of personal conviction. Personal conviction, on the one side, and scientific proof, on the other, do not cancel one another out. Proof is everyone's possession, conviction is one's own. Science may or may not eventually support such a conviction, but it can only do so in its own time and by its own methods. If it does so, it may not be for many years, even many generations.

The present-day prestige given to science has created an image of it as being always in the forefront of knowledge, as always leading the way to new discoveries. It is well to remember that it also possesses the opposite facet; science is cautious, hard to convince, and takes an extremely conservative view towards hypotheses which are not supported by clear-cut observations. Without doubt, the proper role of psychical research is to be thus ultra-conservative. It will tend to follow only very slowly the vivid apprehensions which can be gained by other, private, non-scientific approaches to evidence of survival; in this field science is the tortoise, not the hare. This particular hare and tortoise may reach the same finishing point in the end or quite different ones; but if the former, they will certainly not reach it at the same time.

What then do personal private evidences of survival offer, and what difficulties, rewards and obscurities are found in them?

PART THREE

Search

CHAPTER SEVEN

Difficulties in Personal Evidence

I

WE COME then to each man's personal quest. To the common pool he contributes his own small quota of unique evidence – uniquely received, uniquely interpreted. "Save his own soul he hath no star". The value of the survivalist contribution, built up out of the experience of the many people who have preceded each enquirer upon the same road, is hard to assess. It often makes hasty generalisations and unsound assumptions, but parts of it have sound pragmatic value; for many people have had to deal already with the difficulties, and they can learn from one another.

The newcomer, although normally much less highly trained in judgment than a scientist, is seldom in doubt of his own ability to weigh his evidence. He is not called upon, of course to make judgments which are of a scientific order. The value of his contribution, as we have seen, lies in his evidence being personal to him; he is embarked primarily upon an experience, and upon his own assessment of it. He is his own unique instrument of reception, with which to entrap those particular aspects which elude science. The danger comes when he tries to give it a value of a kind which it does not possess, when he fails to assess its limitations as well as its strengths.

2

What is the newcomer likely to find, then, at his first sittings, and how should he behave? From now on it will be sometimes more convenient to drop the qualifications attached to the language of psychical research – the purported communicator, the soi-disant posthumous personality, and the like. When the communicator is spoken of as if he is who he claims to be, the qualifications must be inferred where they are needed.

The first factor and the one most neglected outside psychical research obvious though it is, is to be sure of what the medium really has said. It is most important to take verbatim notes of every sitting. Memory is notoriously indulgent, and wish and expectation on the sitter's part often lead him to believe that his evidence is stronger than it really is. It may also lead him to suppose that a communicator has said things which support the listener's existing points of view. A careful record may show quite otherwise. Recollection too, even if at first relatively accurate, becomes altered and falsified with time. A single word, a conditional tense, for instance, falsely recollected as an affirmative one, can create a prophecy which in fact was never made. Things which seem irrelevant or insignificant when first heard become forgotten. If recorded, they may subsequently be seen to have held a meaning unsuspected when received. The sitter without accurate records leaves himself on very shifting sands.

One of the most optimistic beliefs of human nature is that it has the power to approach new experiences with an open mind. This is an almost impossible thing to achieve. Confronted for the first time with a medium, it is extremely unlikely that any enquirer will have an open mind. He is almost certain to be unduly suspicious or unduly credulous. It is better to expect that it will take him some time and some experience before he can achieve even a relatively open mind, and this usually only means a mind where existing beliefs, prejudices and expectations will have a modest ability gradually to alter themselves. Moreover a first sitting is usually approached with little idea of its difficulties or of the complicated and delicate processes really involved.

For communication is a fragile and finely poised act about which we still know little, and which can be easily disturbed and shattered. It contains many difficulties and, at times, severe limitations. Every sitting contains the three elements of sitter, medium and communicator; it must be emphasised that all three are constantly contributing to the results, which will largely depend upon the degree to which the three are in harmony. Such alignment, since human factors make it up, can never be perfect. The sitter himself may inhibit the results unconsciously. The medium may grasp the communicator's intention imperfectly and express it wrongly; it may become distorted further still through inattention on the listener's part. Psychological disharmony between sitter and medium is likely to bring about misunderstanding, and, indeed, direct errors in communication, and it is likely to confuse the communicator also. Allowance must be made for the imperfect nature of all sittings, as we know them at present.

Many imponderables influence the success of a sitting; the general harmony of temperament between medium and sitter, and the particular harmony of mood which may or may not prevail at the time of any particular sitting; the extent to which the sitter's mind is agitated by or engrossed with personal preoccupations; the surroundings in which the sitting is held; the health of the medium; even the weather and the time of day. Many sittings exact a heavy toll of nervous energy from the medium; if the medium has been oversitting, evidence tends to diminish, or fail altogether. One sitter will get excellent results with Mrs. A., and nothing at all with Mr. B.; another finds just the reverse; the sitter so pleased with his first sitting may repeat it and get a total failure. Even the best of sittings can be interrupted by erroneous and irrelevant patches. The flow of material is a little like a mountain stream, which brings down with it from time to time mud, stones, branches and other debris, which form no real part of the stream; then it begins to run clearly again.

The enquirer aware of the limitations inherent in sittings will obviously be likely to judge them more objectively than one who comes with preconceived ideas that if the communicator claimed is really present, he must have known this thing or would undoubtedly have said that thing, who arrogantly makes his own rules of evidence without studying what is possible.

3

At the commencement, the sitter will naturally understand very little of these practical difficulties; his early sittings are an apprenticeship. Demands upon the communicator of a kind which ignore these difficulties will in a wise sitter be gradually replaced by others which spring from his growing understanding of mediumship. He may come at first with evidential requirements which are all but impossible to fulfil. Evidence, if all goes well, is likely to come to him. It is wise then at first to leave the initiative to the communicator, to let him build up his evidence in his own way. It requires practice and skill to decide whether to head a medium away from what seems at first to be a false trail.

Sitters are very frequently advised by their communicators to follow as best they can what is being said and to keep their critical analysis until after the sitting, when it can be brought into play as freely as desired.

Control of the sitting should, and does, lie much more with the communicator than the sitter; indeed the degree of this is one distinguishing mark of a good sitting. This is the contrary of what a sceptical investigator often aims at.

Obviously the sitter will volunteer as little information as possible. If he is indiscreet, he will negative the very evidence which the communicator may (or, equally, may not) be about to attempt, and thus make it impossible to know whether the communicator really could have produced it. Questions asked of the sitter should be answered as briefly as possible, without adding any further facts. If asked, "Have you lived in the West Country?" it obviously helps no one if to his "Yes" in reply the sitter adds "In Barnstaple for ten years from 1945 onwards".

He will be guarded; he may go beyond this and be suspicious; what he feels is his own affair, but suspicion is an attitude likely to make a free flow of material difficult, just as it does on ordinary social occasions.

In this very delicate intercourse, the sitter can create mistakes by his own over-credulity, which often brings about a misinterpretation of what the communicator really is saying. Or he may decide, on the contrary, to try and trick the communicator; if he does he will very likely succeed. Close cross-questioning often leads to confusion, as do abrupt changes of subject, or sudden demands for unrelated facts. Many a sitter has probably destroyed gradually unfolding evidence in this way. He then bears the blame for tangling the slender threads which hold together communicator, medium and sitter. For, as we shall see later, communicators may be confused in memory, or struggling with difficulties in the process of communicating; nothing is gained by the sitter adding to them.

The sitter who is patient and courteous to his communicator, who plays fair, and shows a reasonable trust usually receives the best evidence. Lip-service is not enough. No living person is at his best when his listener is mentally placing him in the dock; judgment is needed to decide when it is necessary to put the communicator there.

It is better not to expect or demand some special communicator. Experience suggests that sometimes expectation, far from bringing about the desired communicator, can prevent it. Unexpected communicators turn up, especially in early sittings, and often at the start of sittings. It is better to accept them, and let them say what they wish. They may be preparing the way for the communicator more closely desired. Also the best evidence is often that of an entirely unexpected kind, and this, by its nature, must be left to appear of itself.

It is always hard for the inexperienced sitter to accept why, if the communicator is who he purports to be, he cannot readily meet all the demands upon his earth-memory the sitter cares to make.

It may be as well to pause here, and consider some of the assumptions the enquirer probably brings with him to his early sittings.

He naturally tends to assume that his friend, if surviving, will be wholly unchanged. He will assume that everything he himself remembers, the communicator will remember too; actually the latter's selection of memories may be quite different. He may next assume that the communicator's sole purpose in putting in an appearance is to satisfy the sitter's demands for evidence. However, he may encounter aspects of the communicator which he had not known at all when the latter was on earth. Also he may expect his friend to be wholly accessible, in spite of the intervening screen of the medium's mind.

Doubtless it would be more evidentially satisfying if the communicator were to remain for an indefinite period exactly the same man after death as before, but he could hardly be said to be continuing to *live* if this were the case. The sitter may find a new man, as well as the old one familiar to him.

Therefore it is wise to judge the evidence by what is actually presented, rather than by what the sitter thinks ought to have been presented.

4

Let us take an actual example of the kind of early, simple evidence likely to be presented.

The Dawson-Smith Case, from the records of the S.P.R., forms a useful general illustration of good personal communication. It consists of three sittings, two with Mrs. Leonard and one with Mrs. Brittain, all held anonymously. Both ladies are professional mediums. The S.P.R. report states that further material, faulty or inconclusive, was also contained in the sittings, which indeed is very commonly the case.

The extract below follows that printed in *Proceedings* except for very slight abridgment (of no significance) and with the omission of two pieces of good evidence.

The Dawson-Smith Case

Sitting: October 7, 1920. Sitter: Mrs. Dawson-Smith (Anonymous)

Feda (Mrs. Leonard's control): "The communicator says: 'Have you got the snapshots?'"

Mrs. Dawson-Smith: "I have those you sent me before you passed over."

Feda: "He says: 'Ah, but there are more to come. Will you remember what I say? You will laugh over it, and I want you to laugh. Don't forget it. I feel strongly you will get it and you will see what I mean. I am taken in such a funny position'" (Note 1) "He calls you by a funny name" (whispering, "No, no, not that"). "He must mean Mum. Not – well, but the other is nothing. He says he called you Moth – that spells 'moth'" (pronouncing as written) "but he says 'No, no, ask her, she knows, don't you, Moth?'"

Mrs. Dawson-Smith: "It is short for mother."

Feda: "Just a piece of a word. He says, 'Yes, a piece of mother' and he laughs". (Note 2) "He keeps calling 'Eric, Geoff.'" (Feda shouted the two names) "And Eric! He says, 'All right, put that down and I'll explain afterwards!'" (Note 3) "He says you have some books of his with funny language. He was studying them. He says 'I started to learn the two languages. I have dabbled with many, but these two were different. I could speak one fairly well – but I know little or nothing of the other.'" (Note 4) "He is pleased about the memorial. You know what you have put on it. He says 'Something else is being done which you will know soon, not a private one but a public one.'" (Note 5)

1. Verified in December, 1921, when a brother officer brought two packets, one of films and prints. One snapshot made Mrs. Dawson-Smith laugh; he was surf-bathing in the nude, emerging from the surf with a broad grin.
2. Feda wrote Moth in the air. He always called Mrs. Dawson-Smith Moth (pronounced Muth). In writing to her, he always called her Mother.
3. Eric was a boy who died over fifteen years ago – a very dear and close friend. Geoff was killed in the war, and had been a great chum.
4. Swahili vocabulary. He started later to learn Somali, but had not time to do much before death.
5. A white marble tablet has been erected in Mrs. Dawson-Smith's church in memory. A public memorial, subsequently verified by letter from Nairobi, 12.3.23.

Sitting: January 10, 1921. Sitter: Miss M. Dawson-Smith (Anonymous)

Feda: "He is pleased about the new photographs. He holds two photos, one in each hand, as if giving them . . . 'There is a photo of me – you haven't got it yet'. It is not a proper photo – he calls it a snapshot. He is trying his best to get it to you. He is going to try and impress the person who has it to send it to you. 'It may take some time, but I think you will get it.' " (Note 1) "He keeps on showing Feda you" (Miss Dawson-Smith) "sitting with sheets of paper, etc." (Description of her in C.O.O. hut in Cologne.) " 'Have you got my little key? You were touching it the other day. As you moved about, you touched the key. And there was an old purse with a receipt in it, a tiny paper. It feels old. I wish you could find it, old, worn and soiled, mixed up with a lot of other things.' He doesn't think you have it. Do find it. He calls it a counterfoil. Try and unearth it. He will be so interested. He knows you have it, a long, narrow strap close to it. 'I noticed that accidentally.' He says this is important." (Note 2)

1. Snap found among ruins after death, and forwarded indirectly by brother officer.
2. Found as directed close to long strap. Counterfoil was a receipt for money paid in July, 1914, to satisfy a German debt, and the receipt became very necessary to prevent double payment. Four years after the sitting it was claimed by a Hamburg firm through Enemy Debt Clearing Office. Documents confirm.

Sitting with Mrs. Brittain, February 24, 1922. Sitters: Mrs. and Miss Dawson-Smith (Anonymous).

Mrs. Brittain: "Here is Frank with a chum called Geoff who was killed in a flying accident. But Frank is the one to be talked about. He says Geoff is not to barge in." (Note 1) "I see Frank in a far country, either India or Egypt or somewhere East – he is surrounded by black men, he is the only white man. He was killed through treachery by a bad black man. He was Commander. He was used to commanding mans, white mans and black mans, many soldier mans." (Note 2) (To Miss Dawson-Smith): "Oh, you are a soldier in khaki, with a funny hat. Frank is laughing and says something about 'Knight of the Garter'." (Note 3)

Belle (Mrs. Brittain's control): "The big boy is very tall – six foot two-three, broad on the shoulder, big muscles, showing not much 'meat' on him, nice high forehead, brown face, sunburnt, the fresh air and hot sun gives him fine colour, nice white teeth, big and wide, firm chin with a little dent in it – do you remember it? He has a saucy smile and laughs – 'Ha, ha!' " (Note 4) "Some peoples call him 'Smithie' and sometimes 'Biff'. I don't know why they call him 'Smithie' because it isn't his name – but they call him 'Biff' because he goes like that" (illustrating boxing). "He goes 'pom tiddley om pom, pom, pom' " (illustrating by slapping hands on knees). (Note 5)

Notes by Mrs. Dawson-Smith

1. My boy had a dear chum called Geoff who was killed in a flying *accident* in England, before he could be sent to France. This was in 1917. Not only are the names given correctly, but the fact that it was an accident – not killed on active service.

2. My son (Frank) was in sole command of the native troops on the Northern Frontier District (Abyssinian Frontier) of East Africa, and he was killed by the treachery of one of his own men after signing a peace treaty.
3. My daughter was an officer in the W.A.A.C.
4. Description is exceedingly good and easily recognisable by all who knew him.
5. This refers to a little joke my boy and girl had in which they always spoke the magic words and beat the time on their knees. *

Here are a number of accurate facts, some known to the anonymous sitters, and two unknown (the existence of the photograph, the proposed public memorial), also an incident of a prophetic kind, correctly attaching importance to the search for the receipt. The evidence given through each medium is different. Many people, if asked to put down upon a sheet of notepaper evidential facts about themselves, might find it hard in half an hour to produce an equally distinctive and vivid set; the reader may care to try for himself.

5

When analysed, however, the record is seen to consist only of a number of fragmentary details. Would Frank Dawson-Smith have been able, at the demand of the sitters, to amplify the account with a great many more facts? Might all of them have been given as accurately? Having already given such distinctive facts, which nevertheless was *his* choice of facts, it might be supposed that other facts would present no difficulty, and that he would be able to produce, readily and on demand, any other corroborative facts the sitters cared to seek. Experience suggests that this is not at all the case. In further sittings he might not do so well. Interest might wane. Sometimes the flow of communication just seems to dry up, after a period of mere repetition of much of what has gone before; the wishes of the sitter can do nothing to resuscitate them; it is as if the purpose goes out of them, and only an empty husk is left. This is disconcerting, and a sitter is sooner or later likely to encounter it. However, in daily life, to re-meet old friends now engaged in wholly different interests can bring a similar disappointment. An eagerly awaited transatlantic telephone call, when it actually comes about, may produce nothing but inept inquiries and greetings.

* *Proc.*, Vol. 36, pp. 300–8.

Because Frank Dawson-Smith could give the distinctive memories he did produce, it does not follow that full and perfect recollection of everything in his life remains in his memory after death. Why should it? During his lifetime Oliver Lodge once conducted the experiment of gathering his numerous family around him, and inviting them all to question him about the past. He failed to remember at all a number of things they spoke of. Gathering up his papers at the close, he remarked to his children that it was obvious that he had been quite unable to prove that he was their father! Frank Dawson-Smith's memories, even if stored in his posthumous mind, may not be instantly accessible, and if accessible, may not be communicable. How much of his own character does he really display? To give more than facts, he would need to go on to things which would require the sitter to participate much more closely in the conversation. It would have to become much more an affair of give and take, in which both sides are active, and not he alone. For the Dawson-Smith communication is a one-sided contact. The stage is wholly taken up by his own presentation of evidence. The sitters adopt the course recommended in this book, and allow the communicator to paint his own picture. They rightly refrain, evidentially speaking, from making more than a minimal contribution. Strict evidence, however necessary, can now be seen to become a limiting factor also. In order to obtain it, the sitter has to put a distance, a barrier of reserve between himself and the communicator.

The situation changes significantly as soon as the sitter wishes to pass beyond the role of sifter of evidence, with the curbs it puts upon the tongue. Then a more true, though less evidential, kind of communication begins. It implies at least a presumptive and provisional belief in the reality of the communicator who has established himself by evidence already given. You don't hold true converse with a question-mark, or a dummy, or with what you really believe to be some living person's subliminal mind; at most you interrogate, or you humour. Real converse makes demands on both sides, implies that two sentient beings are facing one another, calls for an equal activity from sitter and survivor. The first thing which follows such a change of purpose is often a noticeable freeing of some, though by no means all, of the difficulties which seem to hamper the survivor. Talk becomes more natural and free on the communicator's side as well as the sitter's.

The sitter is now faced with subjective judgments which go beyond the bare bones of facts, judgments of a kind from which, as we have seen, psychical research has largely to divorce itself. Is a real, independent personality before him, and not only some artefact built up around facts drawn from his own mind by telepathy; something more than an aspect of the medium's self combining itself with facts thus filched? The sitter's judgment has to deal with imponderables. It does not set aside the scientific judgments of psychical research, it operates sooner or later in a different realm, and then comes to a different type of judgment. Different men give different weight and value to these realms. Some will always feel that true assessment of posthumous personality can only begin when the limitations imposed by factual evidence can be surmounted, and a more flexible approach begun.

6

If true converse does take place, we are confronted at once by a most important question: what reality can lie in a posthumous relationship? What purpose can it fulfil?

If Frank Dawson-Smith had escaped his early death, then in the course of time a natural change in his relationship with his mother could have been expected; a partial going-away from her, the growth of new involvements through his career or by marriage. An unchanged relationship with his mother might well have taken on some neurotic or unhealthy aspect.

The change of death is much greater than this natural growing-away implicit in the life pattern. In the same way, if a posthumous relationship is expected to be unchanged and unchanging, it may equally prove to be unhealthy. This may easily happen if a sitter demands at every sitting unchanged emotional satisfactions from the communicator. If the relationship to his mother *is* to remain unchanged, it is hard to justify the return of Frank Dawson-Smith unless it is brief, and attempts nothing more than to bring to her a conviction of his survival. Ought such a contact to cease willingly from both sides once a tragic farewell has turned into a consolatory and reassuring one? Once the threads of affection have been shown to continue, ought they to be rightly resumed in a direct relationship only when the mother has rejoined her son?

It is said without equivocation by some mediums' controls that in many relationships such a reassurance is all that is wise and that each side should then part, and follow their respective paths.

If, however, the survivor does elect to stay close to those left behind, it is surely right to expect that this stay, to be justified, must involve an essentially new and growing relationship.

On what can a new relationship be built? It is seldom that the sitter on his side can help in any problems which belong to the communicator's posthumous life, for how can he enter into the latter's new environment? There can be retrospective problems, a tangled earth-relationship to resolve. That indeed is one most useful task in communication, the bringing together of hurt and estranged parties. A lifting of burdens can result, the resolving of guilt, explanation of misunderstood actions and motives.

When on the other hand a truly new relationship is being forged, the communicator often tries to help the sitter's earth problems. Almost at once the sitter tends, consciously or unconsciously, to exploit it. He seeks help where he clearly should not. "Shall I sell those mining shares?" is a type of question, perhaps all too common, which many sitters do not discipline themselves against asking. The answer surely should be, and indeed usually is, "I can't give any help in such matters." Yet on a more subtle level, is not any kind of help in essence some sort of intervention and therefore perhaps wrong? Moral issues at once raise their head.

Perhaps the communicator gives moral support, proffers advice on emotional, psychological, or spiritual levels. If he has access to a longer sight than on earth, perhaps he forecasts probabilities which look like and are sometimes mistakenly assumed to be prophecies.

If such a one-way flow comes about, with the help all coming from the survivor to the sitter, it is hard for the recipient not to take a selfish role. Here, too, lie seeds of corruption. It can easily become as unhealthy as a merely static, retrospective relationship would have been. For it has a missing element. To be wholesome the sitter must make an outgoing use, an unselfish use of the help given. He must not only make use of it for his own benefit.

Sooner or later he has to ask what the communicator's present task on earth is, and whether it is his own job to share it and help fulfil it.

If he does succeed in doing this, then from being a recipient, he turns to becoming a collaborator. He and his communicator become partners in impersonal work, its value depending upon the communicator's insight, and the sitter's discipline. But what if the sitter is a busy-body or a nincompoop? What too if a long period of time must elapse before the communicator acquires any worthwhile wisdom, a period which may well outlast the sitter's remaining lifetime? Working together does not absolve either from human weaknesses: it may accentuate them. It becomes clear why it is best for many people to cease communicating as soon as they have become assured of survival. It is easy for the sitter to become inflated with self-importance, to take up some task never intended at all by his communicator, and to surround it with a false glamour.

7

Another factor now makes its appearance over and over. It is found that the original communicator gives way to another of quite a different kind. If the communicator cannot himself play a creative role, another personality tends to appear who does. The sitter is led to a mentor. The relative sometimes seems to play little more than a bridging role. It is with the new personality that the sitter finds his real business lies. Sometimes he has a curious feeling that the new communicator has in some sense been waiting for him. They begin to work together, if the sitter is willing.

Now the first objective in their common task usually proves to be very close to hand; it is the sitter himself. In time this dawns upon him. Whatever the sitter may think, the task will not consist of furthering his private interests, in the sort of way in which members of a family unite and support one another against the rest of the world, against all comers. He comes to realise that the communicator's interest in him has a strongly impersonal side. It contains an element of Socratic midwifery; it is essentially a relationship of teacher and pupil. Attention is directed towards overcoming the sitter's limitations, and in helping him to acquire a vision beyond them. The task shared becomes an adventure in consciousness; its purpose is to intensify the sitter's awareness, to sharpen it, and to turn his gaze outwards from himself. A sitter orientated only towards his personal self, who supposes constantly when he sits that "he will hear of something to his advantage", simply falsifies the situation. For the relationship intended is an impersonal and spiritual one; that is where its fascination lies. It can be of enormous service to the sitter, but that is quite another thing than his self-interest. He will be tested, often without recognising it. For what the communicator is trying to say will often be misunderstood; it will tend to be mis-translated into terms of the sitter's old values, instead of intended new ones. The sitter is slowly receiving a new education.

8

In all communication, one thing stands out as extremely important. This is truth of motive. The sitter who comes from self-interest, or from emotional dependence, or for any other unworthy reason, finds in time, almost certainly, that the messages themselves begin to be inaccurate or misleading. He does not always recognise that the cause, in part at least, lies in him. In a subtle way his falseness disturbs and distorts the line of communication; every medium comes to know and likes to avoid this sort of sitter. Selfishness, vanity, greed and ill-will in the sitter distort the processes of mediumship; good motives help to clarify it. Mere good intentions are not enough, for they may mask foolishness and other errors even if the undiscerning sitter pins upon them different labels; some expect miracles, some impatiently expect no result at all. When the sitter fails in integrity, a failure in communication will probably result, just as it often does in ordinary human dealings.

The danger is not all on the sitter's side. Without question some communicators are undesirable. They flatter the unwary sitter or play upon other weaknesses in him, they will confuse and cheat him, attempt to send him on foolish journeys, on missions which have no relevance or purpose. Just as the sitter can falsify and corrupt the intended meaning of the communicator, so must he make sure of the communicator's own intentions. If when in need of advice a person were to ring up the first telephone number which came into his head, and then proceed to carry out blindly everything the unknown voice at the other end suggested to him, he would not be acting less wisely than some sitters do when they visit a medium.

The sitter's true safeguard is to ponder well on any advice given, but never to act on it unless he finds an inner conviction of his own rising to tell him to do so.

The more the sitter brings of himself, his alertness, his own truth and integrity – in fact, the more perfect his own instrument of perception – then the more readily he finds his way through the unrealities and errors which he will certainly encounter. A spiritual partnership between sitter and communicator is not forged without effort or danger. The sitter has to be prepared to be his real self, as far as he can realise that self, otherwise he would do far better to abandon personal communication and its problems altogether.

CHAPTER EIGHT

Difficulties of Communication

I

THE discarnate communicator has several possible ways of approach to the medium. When the latter remains conscious, he attempts to impress his meaning directly upon her mind, often having to make use of visual images and symbols instead of words. The medium then has to pass it on to the sitter as well as she can, it being her own responsibility to interpret the meaning aright. In trance work the communicator's message is often first conveyed by him to the medium's control or guide, and then relayed by this control who is purporting to make use of the medium's mind and vocal organs.

By the first, the conscious method, there is interposed between the sitter and communicator the screen of the medium's mind with all its limitations. By the second method the screen becomes a double one, involving the control as well as the medium.

Alternatively the communicator can himself attempt to take the place of the control and speak to the sitter, but experience suggests that for a time at least he may often become confused and not do so well as a control who is already familiar with the procedure.

Whatever the means chosen, communicators invariably say that the process is far harder than it appears to be. One of the most interesting features lies in the accounts they themselves give of the difficulties which they experience in making their meaning clear.

However wax-like and malleable the medium's mind, however sensitised in receptivity, however quick and resourceful, communicators frequently say that to them it has an almost intolerable insensibility to what they wish to impress upon it. Thus the posthumous Myers:

> The nearest simile I can find to express the difficulties of sending a message
> – is that I appear to be standing behind a sheet of frosted glass – which blurs
> sight and deadens sound – dictating feebly – to a reluctant and somewhat

obtuse secretary. A feeling of terrible impotence burdens me – I am so powerless to tell what means so much.*

The impression is given that speed of thought increases greatly after death, and often cannot be slowed down enough to be caught by the medium even when she is at her most receptive. Myers says to Mrs. Willett, one of the best amateur S.P.R. mediums:

> Let thoughts flit past you. Cease (seize) what you can ... In my eagerness ... the thoughts come so quickly that they slip past you and you do not grasp any one quite clearly.†

At times the communicator appears to find the same difficulty when giving a message to a trance control to pass on; for the mind of the control, *whilst it is operating* upon the medium's mind, seems in some way to become slowed down by it. The control Feda describes the difficulty:

> ... He might plainly tell me, but I might not catch it. At nearly every sitting there is something which Feda knows she has not caught. It is like losing something and not being able to pick it up again. Communicators seem unable to repeat, or else it is that Feda can't catch the repetition.‡

Communicators, however curious it seems, appear to have little means of knowing how far what they have said has got through to the medium.

The Rev. John Drayton Thomas is a communicator aware of this difficulty:

> ... I am not always aware what Feda says when in control. I am mentally following up what I am giving and so am not always noticing what she says. Thus I am not clear as to whether she has given my thoughts rightly or wrongly. As when telephoning, if a slip is made you may not realise how it has been understood at the other end, and not knowing that an error has occurred you cannot rectify it.§

2

Every medium's mind, apart from the inevitable slowness and dullness of reception complained of by communicators, has as well its own particular personal incapacities, insensitivities, incomprehensions

---

* *Proc.*, Vol. 21, p. 208. † *Proc.*, Vol. 43, p. 129.
‡ *Proc.*, Vol. 38, p. 70. For this and other references from *Proc.*, Vol. 38. See also *Life beyond Death with Evidence* (C. Drayton Thomas).
§ *Proc.*, Vol. 38, p. 64.

and emotional blockages, all of which may make it reject part of the communicator's meaning or be impervious to it.

Myers, the impatient, constantly scolds the medium, Mrs. Holland:

> I feel as if I had presented my credentials - reiterated the proofs of my identity in a wearisomely frequent manner - but yet I cannot feel as if I had made any true impression upon them (i.e. the persons he was trying to reach through the medium). Surely you sent - what I strove so to transmit - Your pride if you name a nervous vanity pride (?) was surely not strong enough to weigh against my appeals - Even here under present conditions I should know I should thrill responsive to any real belief on their part - Oh it is a dark road.*

On another occasion, more impersonally he says:

> Imperfect instruments imperfect means of communication. The living mind however sensitive - intrudes its own conceptions upon the signalled message - Even now my greatest difficulty is to combat the suggestions of the mind whose hand writes this though the owner tries to be passive - Short of trance conditions which are open to even graver objections the other mind is our greatest difficulty. And they tire and flag so soon.†

Again, referring to the responses and scruples in the mind of an intelligent medium:

> If one could only find a *stupid sensitive* but the very quickness the impressionability that enables the brain to perceive an influence from afar renders it an ever-present danger to the message that is trying to be impressed. Anxiety to help - fear of unconscious cheating or of self-deception all cramp the hand and impede the willingness to give time and a *quiet* mind to this . . .‡

The *modus operandi* employed seems sometimes to need to be very cumbersome.

> . . . We communicate an impression through the inner mind of the medium. It receives the impression in a curious way. It has to contribute to the body of the message, we furnish the spirit of it. In other words, we send the thoughts and the words usually in which they must be framed, but the actual letters or spelling of the words are drawn from the medium's memory. Sometimes we only send the thoughts and the medium's unconscious mind clothes them in words.§

The following shows something of these difficulties met by a communicator in getting his meaning understood. The medium is attempting a script from inner dictation.

* *Proc.*, Vol. 21, p. 236.   † *Proc.*, Vol. 21, p. 242.
‡ *Proc.*, Vol. 21, p. 246.
§ *The Road to Immortality* (G. Cummins), p. 23.

Now another thought
>   Doocalon

No no try again

>   Dewacorn
>   (This word ended in a scribble)
>   Dewacorn

NO DEUCALION
the sound is Dew

>   K
>   LION not Lion

Write it slowly

>   Deucalion

I want that said It has a meaning
The stones of the Earth shall praise thee
That is what I want said it is I who say it and the word is

>   Deucalion

that was well caught
Good Child
That sort of thing makes one feel out of breath doesn't it on both sides.*

3

The medium's mind may rush in to add meaning not intended at all. A thought received can, through association-habits in the medium's mind, send off that mind in quite the wrong direction, so that further matter is added by the medium, embellishing or distorting the true thought. It might be compared to striking clumsily a typewriter key so that two or three adjacent keys rise with it. Mrs. Leonard's control Feda says:

> ... Your father says that he refrains from saying many things which he wishes to give lest they should come though in a distorted form. Feda feels that also; for she does not always make the medium's voice speak as intended. Feda touches something which wakes the medium's mind and then it goes off on its own account ... cannot stop her speaking if what she says is wrong.†

The direct communicator says:

> No one yet understands the unique character of a sitting ... It is a no-man's-land between the two conditions, yours and ours ... Here lies all the difficulty. Medium and sitter are in part working in a condition which is not entirely theirs, and we work in one which is not entirely ours. It is a pooling

* *Proc.*, Vol. 43, p. 120. † *Proc.*, Vol. 38, p. 80.

of resources which creates the bridge. One gets out of one's depth sometimes on both sides.*

Feda, speaking of such times when the medium is controlled directly by the communicator, puts it more forcibly:

> ... In her brain there is some of her own mind, and also some of his ... In controlling it is, what may be termed, a co-operative mind. You see therefore why he cannot, while controlling, think so clearly, or remember so much, as you can.†

May not such a co-operative mind account at least partly for some of the memory lapses and inconsistencies which so rightly trouble psychical researchers?

The medium's mind can become tired, especially towards the end of a sitting, creating a familiar situation described in spiritualistic jargon as "the failing of the power". The Rev. John Drayton Thomas, communicating with his clergyman son, says:

> It is as if the brain were tired out and it is no use struggling with it ... My thoughts wander and I have no grasp ... I feel my thoughts wandering. We notice this when the power goes while we control. When we were speaking through Feda, and it happened, we thought that she was getting stupid. Now we know what it is. There seems to begin a real waking of the medium's mind, an independent movement, and so we get mixed up with things in her mind. The two being mingled it distorts my messages.‡

4

The Rev. Charles Drayton Thomas, a sitter well aware of the researcher's doubts and difficulties, directly questioned his main communicators – his clergyman father, John, and his sister, Etta – on some of these problems, asking how far matter presented by the medium as coming from a communicator can be really extracted from the sitter, consciously or unconsciously, by the medium herself.

> C.D.T.: Feda, how do you distinguish between thoughts coming from the communicator, and those in the sitter's mind?
> Feda: It is a different feeling altogether, very different. I have trained myself to lean towards the communicator and to shut off the sitter ... Your father says, "Even that would not prevent Feda getting a thought and not knowing it was from the sitter, if the latter happened to be willing

---

* *Proc.*, Vol. 38, p. 100.　　　　　† *Proc.*, Vol. 38, p. 88.
‡ *Proc.*, Vol. 38, p. 76.

something very strongly. A sitter might will his thought fifty times and miss, but Feda might accidentally take it the fifty-first time."

C.D.T.: And would not Feda realise from whom it came?

Father: Not unless she were very careful and on the watch for interference.*

Father (controlling): It is easier for us to read your mind when away from here than it would be during a sitting. It is supposed by some that a medium reads the mind of a sitter; but one has only to experiment to discover how difficult it is for us to answer questions. We can sail along giving details quite unknown to you; but if you suddenly ask a simple question which comes into your mind, it presents a difficulty to us. Now if we were reading your mind there would not be that difficulty.†

Etta: It is difficult to explain, but the expectation by you of some particular thing seems to impinge on some very delicate thought-fabric which we are weaving, and spoils it, so that we cannot gather together its threads in order. They become knotted up. So the advice is, go on keeping passive, and do not think of any particular person or thing; that will prevent your thought impinging on ours. Everything to do with our thought is much more delicate and subtle than yours, therefore our thought should impinge on yours and not vice versa. Father says that it would not be wise to rub canvas upon the paints, it has to be done the other way round.‡

Communicators suggest that the contact maintained during a sitting as seen from their end is even more precarious than its obvious uncertainties and momentary and unpredictable confusions make it seem to us.

(Feda) Feda can hear part, and part not, is able to hear some of it today, but not all of it. A communicator has to break off and leave out something which he knows it would be hopeless, or risky, to try and get through. So that often a sitting seems disjointed, fragmentary . . . He does not always know when he has failed to make Feda hear, and goes on with it. Then, if asked to repeat, he may not know what part Feda has not heard, and then there is a muddle . . . He says there is a good deal to learn about it still.§

In a surprising way, communicators seem to be in the dark as to their results. Edmund Gurney is speaking through the entranced Mrs. Willett to the Rt. Hon. Gerald W. Balfour:

Oh he says, Gerald – Oh he says like that. He's calling someone. Nobody answers – he keeps on calling someone. He says Gerald. Oh he keeps on calling. Oh! he says, where is Gerald?
(G.W.B.: I'm here)
Oh he says, does he hear? how can I know that he hears? . . .

* *Proc.*, Vol. 38, p. 94. † *Proc.*, Vol. 38, p. 93.
‡ *Proc.*, Vol. 38, p. 91. § *Proc.*, Vol. 38, p. 69.

Oh, and he says, the waste of material when we keep on hammering at one point . . . only to find that the point had been grasped and that we might have passed on to new matter.

Oh he says, I can't see your mind, Gerald, but I can feel you in some dim way through her. He says, It's a sort of lucky-bag, her mind to me – when I'm not shut out from it.*

Communicators say then that at times they have as it were to get around the medium, and also to get around the control, in order to get through what they want to say, but often do not know how far they have succeeded. Other types of interference too are possible. Most experienced sitters have found occasionally, at some point in a seance, that there arises in them an odd sensation that the communication is momentarily not on solid ground. Just before this occurs, they may have been receiving satisfactory material, and although the mediumistic flow continues, the sitter experiences a kind of inner warning that in some way or other a break has occurred, and that he will be wise to ignore what is being said for the moment. Later on in the sitting he may feel again that all is well. One cause which can account for this sensation that the communicator so to speak has been switched off temporarily, although the medium goes on talking, can be, as we have seen, that the unconscious mind of the medium can be touched off by something said, and introduce an alien flow for a moment or two.

Another cause is thus given by Feda:

> (Feda) After a sitting is over Feda sometimes finds that there has been someone present who did not get in . . . although they had tried to do so. But although they did not get in themselves, some of their thoughts became mixed up with those of the communicator. This often happens when more than one spirit is present and when the communicator is not well known to Feda. It is not always easy to know who is giving the messages.†

Controls also constantly warn sitters that there may occur breaks through the deliberate intrusion of impersonators, mischievous communicators.

> . . . Set out in our path . . . is the cruel phantom of deceit, stealing the treasure from us. Except in the freedom of communication gained through retained guides, it is dreadfully difficult to avoid these astral intrusions. Not long ago I told of the terrible habit of counterfeiting friends; . . . exhibitions of cunning more common than any real spirit's presence.‡

---

* *Proc.*, Vol. 43, pp. 233-4.
† *Proc.*, Vol. 38, p. 70.
‡ *When We Wake* (M. H. Collyer and E. P. Dampier), p. 199.

5

We now come to a much more difficult area where, although we can see for ourselves that some of the things which communicators describe actually do happen, it is impossible to verify the reasons they give to account for it.

Thus, we are told that the act of communication, at any rate when it involves controlling a medium, itself imposes temporary limitations upon the communicator himself, often resulting in a dimming of his real consciousness during the time that he is in touch with the sitter, so that he can only function with a part of himself, and must therefore present an incomplete picture of his whole being. Some communicators claim to reach, not very many years after their death, a consciousness much expanded and quickened in comparison with that possessed on earth. The onus, of course, is upon them to demonstrate that this is so. However, if such a stage is reached, communicators state that they find themselves placed between two difficulties; either this expanded consciousness is retained, in which case the speaker finds his thought is so swift that it eludes the medium's grasp altogether, or else, by some method of which we are completely ignorant, his consciousness becomes dimmed down so that the medium can reach it, but at the penalty of the speaker losing temporarily much of his own new insight.

What is particularly puzzling is that this reducing process does not always seem to stop at the state of mind which the communicator normally enjoyed during life, with thoughts, feelings and memory at the level of earth clarity, but sometimes proceeds further down the scale still so as to reduce the communicator's consciousness, or such part of it as we become aware of through the medium, to a condition inferior to its former normal earth consciousness. This dimness, together with the failure to have full grasp of the memory-chain, is one reason why some psychical researchers think it more likely that this sub-presentation comes about because the medium is really in touch only in a fragmentary way with the memory-contents of living persons and not with the communicator at all.

Let us see what the communicators say for themselves about these difficulties.

> Father (through Feda): I am not as when I am on my own plane, not by any means.

C.D.T.: Could you not come straight here and throw your thoughts to Feda without changing?

Father: I could do my part, but there would be no result from it. I must make myself, for the duration of the sitting, a part of the particular condition. It is a slowing down to something. I am not at my best, even when conditions are at their best ... When I find myself ... in a sitting, it has what I would call a slightly muffling, even a deadening effect on my memory and faculties. I do not see, remember, and feel with the same lucidity as I do when not communicating. I am tuning down too much ... I feel that I am not complete during a sitting. I have not my whole mental power of memory and consciousness, when returning to the spirit world I feel like a man waking from a partial sleep ... When away from here I know more about it.*

Much the same thing is said even more clearly by Sir William Barrett, one of the founder members of the S.P.R., communicating after death to his wife.

Sometimes I lose some memory of things from coming here; I know it in my own state but not here ... When I go back to the spirit world after a sitting like this I know I have not got everything through that I wanted to say ... I cannot come with and as my whole self, I cannot. ... There is no doubt about it I have left something of myself outside which rejoins me directly I put myself into the condition in which I readjust myself.†

He goes on to try and explain the apparent difficulties of recalling memories:

When I am in my own sphere I am told a name and think I shall remember it; when I come into the conditions of a sitting I then know that I can only carry with me – contain in me – a small portion of my consciousness. The easiest things to lay hold of are what we may call ideas; a detached word, a proper name, has no link with a train of thought except in a detached sense; that is far more difficult than any other feat of memory or association of ideas.

If you go to a medium that is new to us, I can make myself known by giving you through that medium an impression of my character and personality, my work on earth, and so forth. Those can all be suggested by thought, impressions, ideas; but if I want to say "I am Will", I find that is much more difficult than giving you a long comprehensive study of my personality.

"I am Will" sounds so simple, but you understand that in this case the word "Will" becomes a detached word. If I wanted to express an idea of my scientific interests I could do it in twenty different ways. I should probably begin by showing books, then giving impressions of the nature of the book and so on, till I had built up a character impression of myself, but "I am Will" presents difficulties.‡

* *Proc.*, Vol 38, pp. 64–5.
† *Personality Survives Death* (Lady Barrett), p. 55.
‡ *Personality Survives Death* (Lady Barrett), p. 105.

This difficulty in conveying a proper name, and one way of overcoming it, appears in a Geraldine Cummins script, where the control wishes to give the name of Ambrose Pratt.

> I must try and get his name. He shows me the letters Electron. He says it is a foreign word. It is Greek and means Amber. Now he shows me a rose. I see what he means: his name is AmberRose. He makes a little fish, a Sprat. Amberose Prat. He cuts off the sign of S. He makes it clear his name was Amberose Pratt.*

Through automatic writing Myers says:

> Your soul is only aware of those beings who possess bodies vibrating with the same intensity – that is, unless he puts himself into a state analogous to that strange sleep known as hypnosis. When thus conditioned he may go back, temporarily descend a rung of the ladder and make mental contact with a soul who inhabits a denser shape ... and come into touch with human beings. He is thereby frequently caught in the dream of the earth-personality; and it is as if the memory of his experiences on a higher plane were temporarily anaesthetised away.†

It has already been said that if a communicator prefers not to be drawn back too far, and thus suffer the dimming of consciousness already described, he is faced with the opposite difficulty. If he retains his full consciousness, or nearly so, how is he to raise the medium's consciousness temporarily nearer to his own so that she can take his meaning without herself losing the power of recalling it when she regains her own normal state?

> There is a difficulty of margin – Today one touch would draw you so deeply within our influence that the result would be nill for others you would be unable to record or carry back ... and I want them to understand that I purposely hold you away – at arms' length as it were so that you may record.‡

6

Finally there is the difficulty that one who has been dead for a considerable while may be quite unable to convey much of his present state of consciousness to living persons simply because they would fail to understand the changes which have taken place in it. Communicators speak of this impossibility which faces them, of this further reason

---

* *The Light and the Gate* (Raynor Johnson), p. 126.
† *The Road to Immortality*, p. 59.
‡ *Proc.*, Vol. 43, p. 133.

why they have to leave out of the communication much of what they now really are.

> His awareness . . . has vastly increased, but usually he cannot convey a sense of it to those individuals he may endeavour to contact if he chooses once more, like Orpheus, to go down into Hell in search of the beloved. These remarks will explain why so few ever receive any spontaneous impression of the departed. Indeed men and women are as ghosts to us, and only when they seek us with faith and with love do they obtain any convincing suggestion of ourselves, or our earth-personality. Such search is legitimate and will neither hurt nor distress the one who is summoned or sought.*

The communicator, then, sometimes would seem obliged to face entering into some kind of artificial condition in which his earth memories may be no more than a husk assumed temporarily and with difficulty in order to gain the sitter's attention and belief. The sitter after all is usually demanding that the communicator shall appear as somebody who, speaking truly, no longer exists, that is to say as his old earth self.

The sitter only too often from the communicator's point of view insists that the latter shall, in Myer's phrase, "present his credentials . . . in a wearisomely frequent manner", i.e. give evidence of himself, over and over again, because it can be a very slow process for the sitter to allay his own fears of being deceived by, or deceiving himself over the evidence. The sitter constantly goes over the same ground again, doubts, and then reassures himself mentally and emotionally with what to the communicator with his quickened mind must be unbearable hesitations.

On his side, a communicator so often says that the difficulties are surprisingly greater than he could conceive of whilst alive. Inability to control the mediumistic process, ignorance at times of how much of his message has actually come through to the sitter, the voluntary or involuntary limitations which dim his own mind during the actual process of communication, and the apparent temporary separation from the most active part of that mind: if these are true, small wonder that the posthumous Myers complains that it is a dark road.

Cannot a way be found between these difficulties? Can they be overcome gradually? We simply do not yet know – nor perhaps do our communicators – how far these limitations have essentially to be accepted, or how far they can be lessened by mutual experiment.

* *The Road to Immortality*, p. 59.

Experiments, however, they say they do actively carry out.

> ... much is unknown to us even and you are all far behind us in knowledge ... Experiments are necessary here as on earth constant experiments with machines no two of which are alike. ["Machine" is the rather strange word sometimes used by this communicator for a medium] ... The very active branch of our work this side is the experimental branch.
>
> The faculty should divelop (*sic*). It is but little understood so far and we must experiment to find out upon which lines it will best come to maturity.
>
> ... There is an awful danger in your thinking, a heap of you, that the learning stage is so much over now that you can think you have precedents, can lay down rules, and that sensitives can be standardised. Whereas, as a matter of fact, there are many varieties, and you can't lay down canons, you can't bring them up to a standard. You have still much to learn, so have we ...
>
> No one is so overpowered by my ignorance as I am, – I, Myers. Every machine is different, and experience is the sole instructor.*

Particular note must surely be taken of the emotional concern, the disappointment, impatience and occasional satisfactions which communicators give every appearance of suffering. The very difficulties, and the emotions with which they are met, add to the essential realism of purpose with which, despite all their confusions, these messages at times appear so transparently suffused.

These accounts of their difficulties given to us by communicators suggest, sometimes very strikingly, that reasonable truth-seeking intelligences are indeed at work trying to reach us.

* *Proc.*, Vol. 43, pp. 158–60.

CHAPTER NINE

The Medium

I

A MEDIUM is sometimes pictured as a motherly old soul in musty velvet, lying in wait behind a bead curtain. Of course this is a cliché image. Most mediums, it is true, are women, but quite a number are men; amongst those working in recent years have been a stockbroker, the chairman of a large London Building Society, an editor, a printer, an industrial consultant, and a crane-driver. The one thing which all mediums have in common is a sensitivity of an especial kind; this may be combined with crude insensibility at other levels, or may, on the other hand, exist in a personality refined and sensitive in every fibre. There are many modes and levels of mediumship. Indeed each medium is somewhere unique. To generalise, as one must, is to create a very incomplete picture.

The essential qualities of mediumship lie in two things; firstly, in a deep still receptivity, secondly, in the ability to express and interpret faithfully what is received. It is in this sense both positive and negative; it is impossible to draw any sharp line between these; every medium is at times positive, at other times negative.

The particular difficulty of conscious mediumship lies in the double task it has to perform. This sensitivity operates at a level at which a normal person is not aware; after the first task of perception at this level comes the second task of describing what is sensed in such a way that it can be taken hold of by the recipient. The medium has therefore often to transform her material, to translate it from one level of consciousness to another.

It is very hard to hold the thread securely, to keep in touch at the same time with both levels of consciousness.

The posthumous Myers says to Mrs. Willett:

> ... The point we have to study is to find the line where the incarnate spirit is sufficiently over the Border to be in a state to *receive* and yet suffi-

ciently controlling by its own power its own supraliminal and therefore able to transmit . . . We want the operator to be so linked with the mechanism as to control that mechanism herself. We want her also to be so linked with us as to be able to receive definite telepathic . . . radiation. There is one glory of the sun and another of the stars there is the mediumistic gift of emitting and the other gift of receiving.*

Now mediums can choose to work nearer to one end of the scale or the other. The nearer they remain to the level of normal life, the more they will tend to describe communicators as if they are no different at all from the ordinary living persons they once were, and to neglect or to falsify all that is distinctively new in their condition. The true art of the medium lies in coming as closely as possible to the communicator as he now really is. The more she can do this, the richer the contents of her work are likely to be; the less she can achieve it, then everything she says will make the next life seem only a material copy of this, which is the criticism most frequently and correctly made of spiritualistic descriptions. Unfortunately most professional platform mediums concentrate upon the nearer end of the scale; it makes less demands upon their mediumship, they concentrate upon what is easier, because after all, they are paid to produce results. It is what the public wants, or believes it wants. And in the crude psychic conditions of public halls it is very difficult for more subtle types of mediumship to operate.

2

How does a medium, working at public platform level, obtain her material? The process can probably be set in motion by the communicator projecting what he wishes to say into the medium's passive mind, or alternatively by the medium reaching out and taking hold of the material by actively apprehending it with her own mind. It seems likely that it is really a matter of rapport, in which there is often a two-way flow, where either element may momentarily be the stronger. Mediumship is thus reciprocal, in that both communicator and medium contribute to the result though not in unison and often not in full harmony.

Mediums frequently speak of "seeing" the communicator. Quite frequently, though certainly not always, this does not imply any process of visual clairvoyance; it would often be more true to say that

* *Proc.*, Vol. 43, p. 130.

the medium senses the communicator. It is hard to describe this process so as to relate it to everyday living. Let us say that it is possible for a stranger, in an adjoining seat of a darkened cinema, somehow to convey involuntarily to a sensitive neighbour an impression of himself, perhaps of a very unpleasant kind; this impression can go a good deal beyond what can be attributed to direct sense observation. Intensify this process very considerably and apply it to the observation of someone without a physical body and we have, perhaps, some idea of what mediumship at the near end of the scale is like. The medium "feels" a presence, or senses a thought, accurately enough to be able to describe it, and the communicator contributes consciously to the communication thus begun.

Sometimes the medium does indeed see and not sense; but is it then really the communicator that she sees, or is it sometimes only a representation of him of some kind? This might be called the oldest problem in psychical research, for Homer distinguishes between the ghost who is *ho autos*, the man himself, and that which is only *to eidolon*, his image. A medium therefore may sometimes not be seeing the communicator, even though she thinks she does, but only the communicator's picture of himself, some kind of a thought-picture. The picture seen, which appears to possess a certain limited degree of animation, may include some dress or piece of jewellery which the communicator once wore, and which now helps to identify him – but the clothes no longer exist, the jewel may be in possession of an heir. Is the medium then to be supposed to "see" some replica of these trappings, or merely a thought of them, though an accurate thought? And of course if it is only a thought which the medium senses, how be sure it is not the thought or memory of the recipient which is being drawn upon, and not that of the communicator at all? How be sure that there *is* a dead communicator?

This is the danger when the medium remains at the near end of the scale. The need for evidence, intended to bring fact and certainty, may end in doing precisely the opposite, through introducing an element of illusion into the communicator's method of establishing himself. When the medium cannot reach him as he now is, or if the recipient will no longer be likely to recognise or accept him, what can a communicator do but present himself in an illusory form, re-create an image of himself as he was on earth, but an image of what no longer exists? Yet if a medium can only present a mere limited memory-image, the more readily it can be attributed to telepathic reading of a living memory.

A curious fact now emerges. Communicators who resume their earth memories in order to give a message sometimes seem to be overtaken, as it were, by these memories so that in some compulsive way they find themselves temporarily reliving them. In particular they may resume the symptoms of their final illness and transfer these momentarily to the medium, who finds herself, perhaps, gasping for breath, or feels temporarily paralysed, or experiences an acute pain in the heart or chest. This is a very common phenomenon. Here is Mrs. Willett talking to one of her communicators, known to her as the Dark Young Man:

> OH, oh, if I could only remember you when you're gone away. I always forget you. I can't make out how I ever came to know you, and why you will never tell me your name, and why you're so kind to me. That's the man – that's my new friend. He's young and – he's got people belonging to him . . .
> Oh! I fell down, I fell down. Oh! my head, my head, my head. Oh, oh, oh (groans). Oh, oh, oh . . .*

The Dark Young Man, who was a member of the Balfour family and was at that time withholding his name from the medium for evidential reasons, met his death through a fall on Mont Blanc.

These sensations of pain support the idea that much of what is contributed as evidence may be a picture of what the communicator *was*, not of what he *is*. In the passage quoted above, both states seem to appear, the communicator's past sensations suddenly superimposing themselves upon his present self which the medium has been describing.

3

Mediumship therefore makes much increased demands upon the medium when she attempts the difficult task of becoming attuned to the communicator in his present self, with the changes of outlook and resulting intensification of consciousness he may by now have undergone. Courage and intense concentration are demanded of the medium who tries to step beyond the narrow evidential range, and a singularly pure receptivity which must avoid translating whatever she hears into stereotyped earth conceptions, into ready-made moulds of thought.

* *Proc.*, Vol. 43, p. 103.

Mediumship and sitter both come up against this difficulty that the more a communicator changes, the less evidential will his remarks necessarily become. For the medium to apprehend the new outlook of the communicator may be difficult enough, but it may be doubly difficult for the sitter to accept that what is so unfamiliar may indeed be the new communicator; the sitter constantly looks for the old.

At this far end of the scale the communicator's speed of thought is often almost beyond the medium's own reach, and stretches her powers of apprehension to the uttermost. His intended meaning may flash into her brain and must then be immediately slowed down into words, and given forth to the recipient. Mediumship constantly tends towards perceptions swifter than the medium can capture, giving them to a medium a character all their own; it is one way by which she detects their genuineness. One is reminded irresistibly of Shelley's image that the mind in creation is like a fading coal. The medium has to put herself to the extreme limit of her powers of apprehending, without ever quite letting go of herself altogether.

> Oh, I understood that and I lost it. Oh, there is a me that understands what they say, and in handing it on to the next ME it slips and my hands are empty.*
>
> (Gurney speaking):
>
> Lodge, did you notice just now she was so completely over the border (that) though in those instants things swept into her consciousness, she couldn't pass them back; he says I want Gerald to be fully told of this because he says it throws light upon the method ... She projected herself in a rush of sympathy ... put the Primacy of the knowing faculty, and the secondariness of the transmitting, the communicating faculty; the soul's instinctive recognition of truth far out-leaping the possibility of the condensation of it to that point where it can be grasped and framed in language. That's what happened then. We have to keep her at the point where both sides can be touched, but then she let go on your side and by the power of ... recognitive sympathy she broke away and passed, and knew, but could not utter.†

A dedicated medium may train herself towards becoming swift enough to apprehend subtle material without immediately losing too much of it, so as to be then able to go on to choose with full discretion what it is wise to pass on to the sitter, and how best to present it in an acceptable form. The communicator, for instance, may have given to the medium a swift apprehension, *his* apprehension of some truth

---

* *Proc.*, Vol. 43, p. 149.   † *Proc.*, Vol. 43, pp. 131-2.

concerning the sitter's emotional or spiritual condition which, as the medium may equally well sense, it is possible to convey to him only slowly and gradually, because of obstacles in his mind or feelings, or which it may be unwise to speak of at present at all. In such mediumship there is an unspoken element; the medium sees much more than she tells. This aspect of mediumship lies quite outside psychical research; for what the medium chooses to leave untold can form no part of evidence. The medium's task has become much more than a simple relaying of what she sees; it becomes that of interpreter, with all the demands upon her own wisdom which this implies.

4

Mediumship then becomes a great deal more than the messages by the accuracy of which it is almost invariably judged. What it produces as messengership can only be received by the investigator at second-hand. But it must not be forgotten that it is something quite other for the medium; to her it is first-hand experience. Much of the suspicion which exists towards mediums is precisely because their experiences are ones we cannot have for ourselves.

To take a simple example of this first-hand aspect of mediumship; Mrs. Willett finds herself in touch with Gurney, Myers and others of the band of past psychical researchers; through her aid, they pass to us various messages, and make certain general observations. But to Mrs. Willett, there is more; she sees, or rather senses, these dead people for herself. Afterwards she is able in part to tell us how they seem to her, but fundamentally it remains her own private experience.

> I get no impression of *appearance*, only character, and in some way voice or pronunciation (though this doesn't mean that my *ears* hear, you know!) ... I don't feel a sense of "seeing", but an intense sense of personality, like a blind person perhaps might have – and of inflections, such as amusement or emotion on the part of the speaker. If you asked me how I know when E.G. is speaking and not F.W.H.M., I can't exactly define, except that to me it would be impossible to be in doubt one instant – and with E.G. I often know he is there a second or two before he speaks ... I then sometimes speak first ... it gives me no more sense of oddness to be talking to these invisible people than it does to be talking to my son for instance. But I don't think I mentally visualise any sort of "appearance" with regard to them – it is as "minds" and "characters" that they are to me, and yet *not at all* intangible or not-solid realities.*

* *Proc.*, Vol. 43, p. 52.

These "minds" and "characters" display emotions of their own towards the medium.

> I was at dinner when I felt a strong impression of F.W.H.M. scolding me. I can't explain – but I felt disapprobation and felt it coming from him, and that he was wishing me to know that there was no need for any anxiety. I had the impression that he was conveying to me that if I doubted the impression I was receiving I was to try for script after dinner.*

Sometimes it is old private emotions of their own, which the very act of communication resuscitates, as a living person's feelings might be resuscitated, say, by a bundle of old faded letters; then as the communicator feels it, it sweeps in turn over the medium too.

> ... Oh, how my heart aches – Oh, I'm in where there's been such awful grief, and I can feel the old pain streaming all over me. It's someone else's pain. It's just heart-breaking. Oh, Che faro senze Euridice ... †

Here the medium was tuning in to someone she had never known, a dead husband who was recalling his grief, when alive, at the early loss of a much-loved wife. The medium here participates in his old memories with something of his own intensity. It also seems possible for the medium to step into a sort of composite essence of the feelings experienced by a whole group of people. Here, for instance, Mrs. Willett is taken in vision to a room in a strange house.

> ... I wandered about ... at first and looked at the pictures, and then I seemed to pass beyond them, as it were, into the spirit of the room – full of remembered peace and happiness and rest – a strange sense of familiarity and homelikeness.
> The room seemed full of unseen presences and of their blessings; it was as if barriers were swept away and I and they became one. I had no sense of personality in the unseen element – it was just there and utterly satisfying ...
> I can't explain at all why the place moves me so deeply with, as I have said, that feeling of coming back after long absence to loved and remembered surroundings.‡

Sometimes the emotions express the extreme difficulty which the communicators find in the act of communication itself.

> ... the passionate desire to return to drive into incarnate minds the conviction of one's own identity, the partial successes and the blank failures and the failures to help. I know the burden of it to its uttermost fraction.
> (Medium's note) There was a terrible sense of struggle – almost of pain.§

* *Proc.*, Vol. 43, p. 105.   † *Proc.*, Vol. 43, p. 107.
‡ *Proc.*, Vol. 43, p. 107.   § *Proc.*, Vol. 43, p. 106.

Thus, whilst her gift is functioning, the medium can at times be living in a world of intensified experience, of which her sitters are quite unconscious, or which is entered upon when the medium is quite alone.

5

As to the recipient's part, it is by talking, sharing, communicating with these beings, indeed it is by *accepting* their reality that it is possible for them in turn to make themselves more real than they possibly can when there is interposed between them and the recipient a stiff screen of evidential doubt. Necessary though this most certainly is at times, it is important to remember that it inhibits as well as reveals. That is where the medium's direct experiences are of such value in bringing out some of the potential riches which lie in communication with the dead. Mrs. Willett's experience probably resembles that of a number of other mediums, although it gains in expression from her own sensitive and cultured nature; it is rich in the direct communication of that experience to us at the very moments when it is taking place; her sort of mediumship is no mere unthinking relaying to the listener, it is a living breathing record of intense experiences.

Through Mrs. Willett we hear these former psychical researchers continuing to express something of their old characters; we hear Henry Butcher, when asked who he is, saying with donnish precision "I am Henry Butcher's ghost"; we see Professor Sidgwick (it much amused Oliver Lodge) apparently fearful even whilst in the act of communicating that the medium was "getting the material from him" in some way without his consent; we see too, the deep moral earnestness which was so central a part of his earth character. We see Edmund Gurney's characteristic humour, and Myers' impetuosity, impatience, and eloquence.

Although the process is unnecessary for simple evidential statements, true refinement of mediumship rises towards sharing the contents of the communicators' minds and feelings at their deepest level, upon the medium's ability to live as fully as she can in *their* inner world. It is far more than the communicator's words which are sought, it is his inner self, his very soul, and this is far less easily come by than his words. The regrets, the despairs and the exasperation of such experienced communicators as Gurney and Myers, their indications to us of how fragmentary is the form in which their ideas have so far reached us, suggest how peripheral is the work even of so sensitive a medium as Mrs. Willett. Mrs. Willett could not hold for long her contact with her communicators, was constantly tending at a sitting to slip back to her normal self where she could no longer perceive them. Ideal mediumship would require that the communicators do not need to make such desperate effort, and this can only be brought about when the medium is able to rise to the communicators, rather than their having to descend to her. Then, it is true, the problem of communication is not solved, it is partly transferred to the medium who now has to convey to living people just what communicators have already found it so hard to impart to her.

It is impossible to understand mediumship without appreciation that it can move between a number of different and rapidly shifting levels of consciousness; the medium may range over a number of levels of insight during the course of a single sitting.

One key to many of the problems of mediumship thus almost certainly lies in medium and researcher alike learning to distinguish the level at which the medium's mind is working from moment to moment. The medium, if trained in Spiritualist circles, usually passes on immediately whatever she finds herself reflecting from minute to minute, however surprising it may seem, because she has learned from experience that totally unexpected items sometimes produce the best evidence. This unquestioning attitude, however, makes it harder for her to distinguish the value of her material when she is not working at her best; then matter may intrude itself from other levels of consciousness without her recognising its source, perhaps from the mind of the sitter, or from the medium's own normal mind; or impulses from some invading communicator may temporarily overlay or supersede those of the communicator with whom she has until that moment been in touch; if so, it is obvious that confusion will arise until the medium recovers her insight at its original level. These are the particular difficulties of the messenger type of mediumship.

The medium who is able to attain control of her material and who has the power to interpret it to her sitter is less likely to mistake intrusive matter from superficial levels. Nevertheless, however perfect the mediumship these errors cannot be eliminated altogether. But they begin to lessen as mediumship moves on to deeper levels.

6

So far we have considered conscious mediumship. Some of a medium's difficulties are lessened when a helper on the communicator's side appears, and acts as master of ceremonies, and still more when the medium undergoes deep trance. But whatever conception is held of the relationship of the medium to her controls, it must never be overlooked that in unconscious as much as in conscious mediumship, the medium's fundamental receptivity at the upper end of the scale is still required, if high quality mediumship is to result. To conceive of trance mediumship as merely a matter of the medium going off to sleep is wholly inadequate; else we could all be trance mediums if we wished. The fruit of trance work is derived from exactly the same delicate receptivity, the same laying aside of the agitations of the normal daily self, and the same self-dedication as is required of conscious mediumship.

It is not always appreciated how constant a penalty a medium pays for her sensitivity, for the delicately-balanced dissociation through which she learns to function. It usually brings with it an extreme susceptibility to noise. To a trance medium when just about to enter or emerge from her trance, a ring on the door-bell may shatter in an instant the delicate contact made, the movement of a chair on the floor may ring out like a pistol shot, unexpected noises from outside the seance room can come like the report of a cannon, with shattering effect upon her nervous system. Mediums whose return from trance has thus been broken by an entirely normal degree of noise in the room have often found themselves physically badly bruised in the solar plexus. A finely attuned medium has a constant struggle to safeguard her sensibility.

Mediumship of real value demands a discipline which is far more than merely putting out one's best efforts whilst actually working. It is quite another thing to undertake the voluntary and unceasing discipline in every part of the being with which the best mediums are faced, the constant stilling and refining of the mind, the refusal of the countless distractions of ordinary life, the ability to remain uncorrupted by power, even petty power, by flattery, money or the illusions of self-importance. True mediumship requires the gradual removal of every quality and thought which can stand in the way of serious communicators, and cloud the receptivity of the vehicle. For without doubt the limitation of the medium imposes in turn a limitation upon her communicators.

Perhaps the purest form of mediumship is that which wholly surrenders itself to becoming the constant vehicle of one who claims to be a guide and teacher. This phase of mediumship is dealt with in the next chapter. Through the years such a medium becomes closely attuned to the consciousness of her guide. As any pupil eventually partly reflects his teacher, so a faithful medium gathers into herself something of the same wisdom that her guide has imparted continually through her, and at times comes to express it directly through her own insight. On the other hand the medium who opens herself to many influences in turn is likely to be obliged in consequence to offer to all a shallower level of consciousness. The demands insistently made on mediums to produce more and more evidence inevitably results in limiting their powers of reaching discarnate beings at deeper levels of consciousness.

Another phase of seership consists in mental travel into the worlds beyond death in order to study at first hand their governing laws. Direct insight then replaces the reflective quality of much mediumship. One such way into these worlds has been outlined by Rudolf Steiner, who gave it the name of spiritual science, and who then demonstrated the correctness of his observations by a many-sided application of them afterwards to practical fields of living.

A number of different doors open into these inner worlds of perception; what is supremely important is the quality of character brought to them, the depth of insight, and the use made of them by the medium or seer.

CHAPTER TEN

The Trance Personality

I

CONTROLS and guides of mediums in trance can be divided into types, according to the functions each claims to carry out. The most common type of control acts as a general communicator whose task is mainly to describe the sitter's dead relatives or friends and to give messages from them. Such controls state they are the reflectors of facts and impressions first derived from communicators and then passed on to the recipient. Familiarity with the process of controlling the medium is said to enable them to do better than the communicators could do for themselves. Theirs is a specialised and limited role.

These controls, of whom Mrs. Leonard's Feda is a good example, remained attached almost but not quite exclusively to one medium. Very often these messengers represent themselves as children and talk in a childish and ungrammatical way. Are they what they purport to be? One wonders; for even with the years, one continues to know next to nothing about them, and certain puzzling and unsatisfactory features appear.

There is for example the time factor; these childish personalities who appear as controls, who sometimes remain with their mediums for thirty years or more, do not give any sign of change, of growing up; the Bellas and Topsies remain much the same children as they appear to be from the first. According to spiritualistic lore, when an earth child dies it will grow up and come to maturity in its environment after death, but these controls do not. The child control does not form a consistent image. Behind the childish prattle, there, sometimes appears, if only infrequently, an unmistakably mature sensibility; feelings and perceptions are produced which are certainly not those of children, and which may or may not be associated with the medium's own consciousness.

These controls, whether children like Feda or adults, are personally unknown to any sitter, and seldom produce any verifiable evidence of their past earth existence. Without doubt, for reasons we cannot fully understand, there is an incompleteness in their presentation of themselves.

Thus Phinuit, the messenger-control during Mrs. Piper's earlier years of mediumship, claimed to have been a French doctor. Researchers who assessed his personality all believed this to be in the highest degree unlikely, for he could never produce any real evidence of medical knowledge, nor did he possess more than a few French phrases. Phinuit, too, was shifty when questioned. He would also fish without scruple for any evidence he could pick up from sitters, but if this was not forthcoming would then proceed to produce excellent evidence without its help.

The M.N. Case

M.N. visited Mrs. Piper in March, 1888. He was told by Phinuit that a near relative would die in about six weeks' time, and that pecuniary advantage would result to him. Subsequently Mrs. Piper, in a sitting, told M.N.'s fiancée that it was M. N.'s father who would die.

The father died in mid-May very suddenly from heart failure, a few hours after his doctor had pronounced him out of danger.

Previously Phinuit had said he would try to influence the father about matters connected with his will.

Two days after M.N., in America, had received a cable announcing the death in England, Phinuit spoke of his father's arrival in the spirit world, and said he had tried to persuade him whilst sick. Phinuit stated the nature of the will, and described the principal executor who, he said, would make a disposition in favour of M.N., subject to the consent of two other executors, when M.N. went to London from America. This proved correct.

M.N.'s sister, at her father's bedside during the last three days of his life, said he had repeatedly complained of the presence of an old man at the foot of his bed, who annoyed him by discussing his private affairs.*

Did someone appear at the bedside at all, and if so was it or was it not Phinuit, carrying out his promise, and at the same time demonstrating on the other side of the Atlantic a separate existence from his medium?

Feda has made a mildly compulsive intrusion very occasionally into her medium's ordinary life. Thus Mrs. Leonard once self-consciously carried along the street a toy balloon which Feda "made" her buy. Feda also occasionally wants to give away the medium's possessions in

* Summarised from *Proc.*, Vol. 8, p. 120.

ways which do not accord with social custom, and once threatened to discontinue her work unless Mrs. Leonard gave away a ring to someone whom Feda wanted to have it. Mrs. Leonard very reluctantly did so, to humour Feda, whose threat after all affected not only Mrs. Leonard's livelihood, but her vocation also. It is very much to Mrs. Leonard's credit that she has been so frank about these incidents. But whatever the ultimate truth may be concerning Feda, Phinuit and their like, we continue to know much less about them than we do of the direct communicators they have helped.

Nevertheless some of these controls, when established, perform their function in a regular and dependable way, with few of the lapses which Phinuit indulged in. Feda in her own way has quite a professional attitude to her work. On the other hand, Feda, like similar child controls, can produce very unconvincing excuses when her failures are pointed out.

It is easy, of course, and tempting to conclude that the control is only a split-off part of the medium's personality. This is discussed in section 3 of Chapter 11.

2

It is, at first sight at least, much more difficult to account in such a way for the next class of controls, who appear during the medium's trance – recently dead people who give excellent evidence of being the people they claim to be, close relatives of Mrs. Leonard's sitters.

Some of these controls, such as John and Etta Drayton Thomas, have graduated from being communicators, known at first only through Feda, and who then gave messages only with her help. It is harder to claim that *they* are split-off parts of the medium's mind, when they can exhibit such clear memories of a recent earth-existence. It would be a strange sort of compulsion of the medium's mind to split itself into the convincing likeness of complete strangers to her, and to go on steadily presenting likenesses of further strangers, as new sitters come to her over the years, all of these strangers appearing to bear no inner relationship at all to her, but to be concerned with minding their own business of giving evidence to their own relatives.

Nor do John and Etta Drayton Thomas ever overlap in the medium's presentation, but preserve separate and appropriate memory streams. Nor are they limited to appearing only when their relatives are sitters.

It is still more difficult readily to confine these relatives to the medium's own self when they go to considerable pains, as did the Rev. Drayton Thomas's father, to explain the difficulties found by him in the process of communication, which difficulties he sometimes expressed when in direct control of the medium, sometimes, as we have seen, with the aid of Feda.

3

We now come to the difficult question of the guide. The guide has a wider role than that of a general control, whose task, as we have seen, is largely limited to assuring that order prevails in the *process* of communication, and in giving evidence on behalf of those unable to communicate satisfactorily for themselves. Guides, on the other hand, are presented not only as teachers of spiritual wisdom but as personages in no way limited to mediumistic presentation, who play a part, whether recognised or not, behind the scenes in every human life.

Nobody is likely to sit long with mediums without being told that he has a personal guide who is in touch with his charge at all times during his life. This obviously does not postulate a constant personal attendance, though doubtless some Spiritualists are convinced that it does, and need not imply more between a guide and his pupil than some contact of a telepathic kind. The pupil, consciously or unconsciously, can perhaps call for help from the guide, the guide may have means of discovering when his help is needed. When the pupil's occupation is trivial – and presumably for a guide this includes nine-tenths of his activities, including most aspects of making his living and of amusing himself – there can be little or no need for the guide's attention. He can only be expected to be concerned with the moments of spiritual significance. The dazzled sitter who comes to assume that a guide, or perhaps more than one, is helping him to carry out his own petty earth desires, and has no other tasks and no other pupils, attributes an importance to himself which exactly reverses the meaning of the relationship as it is really presented.

The concept of a guide is linked with that of each individual life possessing a spiritual plan or pattern, of however provisional a kind, and of the guide's task lying in helping the pupil to fulfil the spiritual opportunities within this plan, and to carry out on earth the tasks appropriate to it.

The enquirer is often told by a medium of his personal guide, perhaps receives a brief description of him, and advice is given said to have emanated from him. Contact with a personal guide has to take place in this way, unless the sitter is willing to undertake the often difficult task of developing his own intuitional faculties in order to make contact with his own guide directly. In practice what a person is taught about his own moral nature is far more often received from the teaching guide of a medium.

Now everyone has the right and the necessity to expect such guides, whether one's own personal guide or that of the medium, to prove, not so much their identity – which after all does not matter very much – but their status and stature by demonstrating it over a course of years. Their pupil is entitled to ask that they show themselves to be familiar with his inner problems, his strengths and his weaknesses of character at a deeper level of insight than can be attributed to the medium as a human person; also indeed – if they are to justify their appearance – at as deep or deeper levels than those offered by doctors, psychologists, teachers, priests, and similar counsellors of dedicated human insight, and long professional training and experience.

Can these guides, therefore, who present themselves through the uncertainties and limitations and mysteries of the mediumistic process, come anywhere near such a standard, much less surpass it?

The real test of these alleged guides must lie in how much wisdom they do in fact impart, rather than by the mode of their appearance. They can be judged by the intrinsic value of whatever they have to say. Guides constantly divorce themselves from any authority based on their own stated origin; they invariably ask to be judged by what they say, and not by its source.

Let us see what strengths and limitations we find when we study these personal guides, and – in the much fuller way in which we can come to know them – these controls who make use of one particular medium year after year for the purpose of providing general teaching.

A difficulty has to be met which is very disconcerting to those who later on come to give value to a guide's teaching. This is the inappropriate and fanciful presentation in which they often appear clothed.

As is well known, the guides presented at sittings make up a colourful, an all-too-colourful array. Hindus, and Arabs, Egyptian priests and Redskins are to the fore, nuns too are fairly common. Some of these only speak muddled nonsense, and are obviously the product of pseudo-mediumship. But as for those presentations which cannot be so easily dismissed, it is very odd, whatever their purpose, that they should choose to make such a fancy-dress presentation of themselves through the entranced medium.

Some speak very imperfect English; if they are what they purport to be, surely a way could be found around this difficulty of language; surely they could master English before they ever take control of a medium? It is curious how a guide's English comes to improve during the years; if he can learn elsewhere, however imperfectly, the rudiments of our language before he first appears through the trance, why does he not wait longer, and defer his appearance until he has learned perfect English? And why can he not use from the start the English, superior to his own, which his medium already possesses? What can we think when we find guides who painfully address staid matrons as "squaw" and comment on their "wigwam", only to drop this thin veneer when the guide comes to know the sitter better? What is to be made, on the other hand, of a Red Indian who talks of epignosis, and who shows himself acquainted with the Oxyrhynchus papyrus?

It has to be noted that some guides refuse to give themselves a name at all, or when they offer some Red Indian or other name, it later becomes clear that its real meaning is symbolic. The name of the guide, Red Cloud, he tells us, symbolises the cloud by which the Israelites were led away from the fleshpots of Egypt, the name chosen by the guide White Eagle is a symbol of the Johannine teachings. How relate these Christian connotations solely to the lightly-sketched Red Indian impersonation? Such a covering, however, may have a use when a name or personality, and the accretion of any authority, are sought to be avoided, or when a guide wishes, as he often does, to discourage the all-too-willing personal attachment which some sitters wish to give. However, it has to be accepted that between the outer presentation of a guide, and the inner character he subsequently demonstrates, there stretches this disconcerting gap. Sometimes the performance is so superior to the outer presentation that it is hard to match the two together.

How much does a guide know about his charge? Odd lacunae show up in his acquaintance with his pupil's outer circumstances. His store of facts concerning the pupil's affairs seems to wax and wane. What to the pupil are obvious facts about himself may appear on one occasion to be unknown to the guide, and yet on another the guide may introduce a very clear reference to them. Guides are certainly not free from the difficulties of communication. Whether or not a guide is a being of wisdom, what is certain is that his knowledge of his pupil is not at all like the facts in a Scotland Yard dossier. It almost seems as if he sees him, not as we see our friends, from without to within, but from within to without. The enquirer, if he is at all sensitive, soon comes to realise that it is pointless to try and test a guide by the setting of little private traps in the conversation, or by treating him as a sort of instantaneous fact-finder who, if his claims are true, "ought" to be able to produce a ready answer to any question. A guide's reality does not reside in the realm of facts: it resides if it resides anywhere in the realm of his consciousness.

4

The first way in which a guide often impresses his pupil is by the knowledge he shows of his character. He shows that he already knows the salient spiritual events in his life, and often looks at them in quite a different light than the sitter does. When the sitter attempts to put a gloss upon his own character and actions, it produces an uneasy feeling that he is certainly not deceiving the guide but only himself. The sitter soon realises, if he has any powers of self-criticism, that he is quite unable to project his own image of himself upon the guide. He has to take or leave himself as the guide sees him, or rather as far as a guide allows the sitter to see how he views him. Guides are certainly not lacking in a humorous charity.

The sitter in turn gradually gains a view of the guide's own character, as it is expressed through the mediumistic trance. He is likely to find him even-tempered, wise, benevolent, far-sighted, tolerant, humorous, patient, and probably extremely subtle. A strong sense of dignity may convey itself, and an authority which is never insisted upon; an impression of great humanity combined with an apparent freedom from the smaller human failings. This is certainly a very great deal to claim. No doubt to many people it is a ridiculous claim.

If however it is true, then guides must be paragons of virtue. Unlike some who are regarded on earth - or regard themselves - as paragons of virtue, guides are altogether delightful companions. Their company is not spoiled but enhanced by the knowledge they show of the sitter's deeper character, and the marked ability they demonstrate to read his unspoken thoughts.

5

Sometimes a guide begins his work by dealing with some great personal trouble, which probably at the same time holds within it the clue to the pupil's greatest need. At other times, the guide prefers to give the pupil a boost, and even comes near to flattering him. That is putting it bluntly: put from another angle, his eye is upon the man's inner possibilities, rather than upon his present performance, but almost invariably the sitter thinks he is being congratulated on what he already is; hence the element of seeming flattery. It is usually only later that he finds that really there has been put before him an ideal he has not yet fulfilled.

Guides sometimes discuss the future; this does not necessarily imply prophecy. It is easy but fatal for the listener to look on an imputed prophecy as bound to occur and therefore as making any hard work unnecessary on his part; to give a goal or an ideal to a man is no prophecy; it is for him to fulfil it or not. The insight of a guide into his charge does at times, however, seem to extend in part into his future; he may show himself aware of, and gradually prepare the pupil for, heavy duties which the latter would otherwise find himself most unwilling to face, or of a coming decisive choice of paths, or of the challenge or entanglement of a relationship which will put stress upon untried aspects of the charge's character. There seems something more than could arise from anticipation based on insight into character, in that it includes at times some advance knowledge of persons and incidents only encountered later on by his pupil.

Work with a guide is a long-term process, seldom consisting of specific instructions to act in this way or that, but intended gradually to widen and deepen the consciousness of the sitter. An outstanding characteristic of any responsible guide is his scrupulous respect for the free-will of his listener; in particular he never tries to impose beliefs upon him, still less to make him dependent upon him. On the contrary, the guide's teaching is frequently directed towards enabling his charge to work without the intervention of a medium, not by developing mediumistic gifts of his own, but by what can better be described as the reaching of an interior awareness of how to deal correctly with his own problems. The guide cannot do the pupil's work, the pupil can only do it for himself. At certain stages, in certain problems, the guide stands on one side; the pupil is left to solve his tasks alone.

6

When addressing a group of people who are at very different levels of understanding, it will be found that a teaching guide sometimes talks at the same time at several layers of consciousness, allowing each pupil to gather what he can at his own level. The Cervantes whom a young man reads is not the same Cervantes he comes to know in his maturer years; some of the earlier meaning has retreated, but the author's work has added to itself layers of meaning now seen for the first time, and which altogether escaped the younger reader. In a similar way, in re-reading a guide's teachings one, five or ten years after they were first studied, the pupil often comes to feel that he is seeing for the first time what the guide really means. He finds it very puzzling how he missed before what is now so clear to him. The teaching of course is the same; it is his consciousness which has moved on, bringing out new layers of meaning missed before.

Most guides, explicitly or implicitly, claim to possess a long term of years, possibly thousands of years. If it is to be taken at all seriously, the possibility of talking to a being who is several thousand years old is a very extraordinary one, and the mind boggles at the amount of experience which such a being, if he exists, must have collected during this time. Will his mind and feelings still be recognisably like those of an ordinary living man? Or will there be an area which is quite incommunicable because beyond the range of earth experience? Will he only be able to talk to us therefore with a small corner of his mind? And how much even of that must inevitably be distorted by interference from the medium's mind, and then distorted again by the listener's own particular set of prejudices, and the misattention which these bring? Either the whole notion of such beings is illusory, or if they do exist they must be expected, if time is not a mockery, to be vastly superior beings to us. On the one hand, if they are indeed illusory, we shall certainly have the power of judging them to be so; on the other, if communication does exist, however imperfectly, with such ancient beings, it is likely that we are extremely impertinent to try and judge them at all. We are confronted with these two widely different possibilities, either that these teachers are utterly chimerical, or else are likely to have a wisdom far surpassing our own.

At present, in order to put himself into a position to make any sort of adequate judgment, an investigator may have to be willing to lay himself open for a while to the intellectual and social mockery of his friends and professional associates, and to risk sharing the company of people without the ability to understand his own mental reservations. For it will rapidly be found that guides value people for qualities which have nothing to do with their intellectual and cultural status.

However if Darwin found it worth while to play his flute to an earth-worm, on the grounds that no experiment can be too ridiculous, it need not be without value to make examination of the claim that ancient beings exist and have found a way of communicating with us.

The value of what is received is necessarily interpreted at the receiver's level; the same words can give more to one person than to another. The investigator has to ask how far his instrument of detection, his consciousness, can encompass the mind he is seeking to assess. The evidence is better not dismissed too quickly, in case it is the human instrument which is faulty, because judging from an inadequate level. For if an ancient being truly is speaking, he can only make accessible whatever part of his mind is beyond the consciousness of his listener by gradually widening the latter's consciousness too. That is why the relationship sought by a guide is always the teacher-pupil one. Like poet and prophet, he will be obliged to create his own audience over a process of time, bringing gradually to listeners the means by which to understand him.

7

It is a pertinent question to ask why there should be any need for ancient beings to help men; why should not such a role be performed, if it is appropriate for it to be performed at all, by much more recent arrivals in the worlds beyond death? Does not the claim that mediums are controlled by ancient beings in itself smack of a desire for self-aggrandisement in the medium, because she wants to make an impression beyond her own intellectual or social status? Why should not one's guides be well-educated men of one's own race, who could be expected to be able to provide a sufficient degree of spiritual guidance based on their own experiences after death, and who could also give practical and technical help to their professional successors on earth? Have we any evidence of such professional men sustaining the roles of technical expert and spiritual teacher?

Now mediumship at present appears seldom able to produce technical matter and, in view of the difficulties found in communicating normal material, this is not surprising.

Sir William Barrett, when on earth, had been interested in certain messages claiming to come posthumously from Sir William Crookes. Barrett, after his own death, states through Mrs. Leonard that he had now found that parts of the messages did emanate from Crookes, but that other parts had been added by the mind of the medium. Now if one were the posthumous Crookes, what would one do? Would one be content to go on giving messages – especially those with a scientific content – in such a diluted form? One might well prefer to refrain from giving them at all, or on the other hand, one might leave mediumship aside and attempt instead to bring to bear a direct telepathic influence upon the minds of living scientists, who would at least understand the meaning of the problems one wished to shed light upon.

If discarnate influence is accepted at all, it becomes impossible to say where mediumship begins and ends. It is a commonplace that some creative minds, artistic or scientific, consider that their ideas sometimes reach them as if they were not their own. This may be the natural process by which a man's own ideas spring up from his unconscious; it does not of course prove any intervention from a discarnate mind; but equally it may be rash to dismiss the possibility that creation can at times include an *element* of participation from discarnate minds, by a more direct route than by mediumship.

8

Evidence of a somewhat dramatic kind, which arose out of the R.101 airship disaster, illustrates some of the difficulties which may face a would-be communicator endeavouring to give technical evidence. The case involves members of the crew who had been killed in the disaster and who then purported to communicate their view of the causes before the official enquiry, and another airman, previously dead, who attempted to give warning before the disaster came about. The whole account is well worth study, for it is a complex case which would tax the most enthusiastic exponents of extended telepathy to explain entirely by that theory.

The dirigible crashed near Beauvais on October 4, 1930, on her first long voyage.

Three days after the disaster, while the causes of the crash were still unknown, through the mediumship of Mrs. Eileen Garrett, a communicator announced himself as Flight Lieut. H. Carmichael Irwin, who had been captain of the airship. He spoke in staccato sentences as though under great difficulty: "The whole bulk of the dirigible was entirely and absolutely too much for her engine's capacity. Engines too heavy. Useful lift too small. Oil pipe plugged . . . Flying too low altitude and never could rise. Disposable lift could not be utilised. Load too great for long flight . . . Cruising speed bad and ship badly swinging. Severe tension on the fabric which is chafing . . . Engines wrong – too heavy – cannot rise. Never reached cruising altitude – same in trials. Too short trials. No one knew the ship properly. Weather bad for long flight. Fabric all waterlogged and ship's nose is down. Impossible to rise. Cannot trim. Almost scraped the roofs of Achy. Kept to railway. At enquiry to be held later it will be found that the super-structure of the envelope contained no resilience and had far too much weight in envelope. The added middle section was entirely wrong . . . too heavy, too much over-weighted for the capacity of engines . . ."

Although neither the sitter nor Mrs. Garrett had any technical knowledge of airships . . . the basic facts communicated were essentially established . . . when on 1 April, 1931, the Court of Enquiry issued its report.

Before the Enquiry, others who lost their lives during the flight, including Capt. Scott, spoke through Mrs. Garrett to Major Oliver Villiers, the senior assistant of intelligence at the Ministry of Civil Aviation at the time, but who was not an expert in the technical factors.

Villiers: What was the trouble? Irwin mentioned the nose.
Scott: Yes. Girder trouble and engine.
Villiers: I must get this right. Can you describe exactly where? We have the long struts numbered from A to G.
Scott: The top one is O, and then A, B, C, and so on downwards. Look at your drawing. It was the starboard of 5C. On our second flight after we had finished we found the girder had been strained, not cracked, and this caused trouble to the cover . . .
Scott (later, when referring to the final flight): Now about the rent in the outer cover. The same place – 5C – this time.
Villiers: Do you mean it actually broke and a piece of the girder went through the outer cover?
Scott: No, not broke, but cracked badly and it split the outer cover . . . The bad rent in the cover on the starboard side at 5C brought about an unnatural pressure and the frame gave a twist which, with the external pressure, forced us into our first dive. The second was even worse. The pressure on the gas bags was terrific, and the gusts of wind were tremendous. This external pressure, coupled with the fact that the valve was weak, blew the valve right off and at the same time the released gas was ignited by a back-fire from the engine.

Among other technical items given by Mrs. Garrett are the following: "Starboard strakes." Strakes is a nautical term denoting the longitudinal plates on the side of an airship. "This exorbitant mixture of carbon and hydrogen is entirely wrong" apparently refers to highly important technical experiments then being contemplated at Cardington, the R.101 base. Another message "Same with S.L.8 – tell Eckener" refers to the identification number of a German airship involved in another air disaster; Eckener was responsible for the Graf Zeppelin. It is also significant that a number of warnings of future danger to the R.101 were given to the widow of Capt. Hinchliffe, who had lost his life on an Atlantic flight two years previously. He spoke to his wife through Mrs. Garrett. "I want to say something about a new airship which is now being built . . . They will start without thinking of disaster, but the vessel will not stand the strain. It will come down one side first. I do not want them to have the same fate as I had. As Johnston was a good friend of mine, I have tried to impress them myself, but it is inconceivable how dense these people are." Johnston was the navigator of the R.101. Hinchliffe's second message said: "I want to speak to you again about the condition of affairs at the airship station. I have been there to impress them. I wish to goodness it was possible for you to tell Johnston in confidence and ask him to be careful. I know what I am talking about." Mrs. Hinchliffe twice went to Cardington, and saw Johnston. He would not pay any attention to the warnings. Hinchliffe's third message said: "I do not think these dirigibles are able to face climatic conditions. They have not the right wind resistance. They are fairly all right until they get to a certain altitude. There is a sympathy with the hydrogen which weakens the tissues where the air combustion gas is kept. You get all sorts of lockings at a certain altitude – you cannot get over it." Later Hinchliffe said: "Johnston will not listen at all, but you will find that he has gone over things. From what I know of atmospherics the whole idea of dirigibles is spending money in vain, for they are not practical. Johnston thinks the airship is all right, but I am very dubious about it. Perhaps nothing will happen on the maiden voyage, but she is not going to last." Mrs. Hinchliffe asked her husband to state definitely whether he was referring to the R.100 or R.101. He replied: "It's the R.101 I mean. Johnston does not seem interested although they have added some new defensive beams. I do not see anything yet happening on its maiden voyage, but there will be an accident to it." The R.101 accomplished her maiden flight on October 14, 1929. Hinchliffe continued to send warnings at intervals right up to the day of the final flight, one of the last messages referring to the danger "in a storm or bad conditions". A few hours before the disaster Hinchliffe said at a seance: "Storms rising. Nothing but a miracle can save them."*

It will be noted that the messages purporting to come from Hinchliffe state that he had attempted to influence Johnston, though in vain, by direct telepathy.

* Based on accounts in *The Enigma of Survival* (Hornell Hart), *The Millionth Chance* (Leasor), *No Living Person Could Have Known* (Neech) and *Quarterly Review of the Churches' Fellowship for Psychical Study*, Mar.–Dec. 1962.

9

In addition to the problem of mediumistic limitations, the transmission of technical knowledge is bound up in a different way with the problem of proof of identity.

Some would not be satisfied with evidence of personal identity unless it were to include some memories of technical matters which had been known to the survivor; the R.101 evidence was given almost immediately after death, but how are we to be sure how long memory of this kind will persist? Some communicators say that earth memories fade very rapidly to unreliability.

If deeply engraved personal memories can be hard to recall, then professional and technical information may also dim in the memory, or their owner's interest in them become diminished; we have no right to demand that once an engineer, a man must continue indefinitely to be an engineer, once a doctor, that he must always remain interested in diseases which may well exist only on earth. Is it not conceivable that as the result of his posthumous experiences over a term of years – which if we can accept Myers's thoughts, as expressed in *The Road to Immortality*, may bring some very fundamental changes of consciousness – some formerly prominent professional man may find that he no longer wishes to impart further technical knowledge to his successors on earth, but is now interested only in making a more fundamental impact altogether on their minds?

Such seems, for instance, the sort of reply, again purporting to come from Crookes, in answer to scientific questions of a general type put recently by Sir Victor Goddard through the automatic writing of Grace Rosher. The answers encourage certain directions of scientific exploration on moral rather than on precise scientific grounds. Evidentially speaking there is little in the material to establish that it is Crookes who is writing, although the handwriting itself closely resembles Crookes's own, and the intrusion of the moral element may of course be attributed to the medium and not to Crookes. Yet, from another point of view, it might be wiser to ask whether the *content* of the answers is fruitful in its context or not; if it is of value apart from the authority of the alleged speaker, it surely does not matter, from one angle, who the real speaker is. This is a fundamental problem of communication; as soon as the possibility of a metamorphosis of consciousness is allowed for, even a partial one, communication in terms of evidence has largely to be abandoned in that particular case. Apart from ability or inability to recall his earth memories, when does Crookes cease to bear unmistakable likeness to the earthly Crookes, when can the posthumous Myers be allowed to outgrow his old self? It is a difficulty of which some communicators are perhaps more aware than is generally allowed.

> I say that the evidence of survival is not easy. The going out of the soul means so often a change of outlook in many things; averring one thing in the body, and when over the border, quite different ideas. They often consider it right, therefore, to keep all reference to a new outlook out of their thoughts ... when coming through. You can ask yourself why you do not get your family much now. Suppose it to be possible they think you would grieve for the personal touch they cannot give.*

10

We are confronted with another very obvious problem. Communicators, controls, guides, all presumably display something of their present selves with the help of, or in spite of, their medium, but *how much* of these present selves?

We have seen that articulate communicators such as Drayton Thomas and Barrett say that in order to communicate with us they are compelled to leave something of themselves outside the process altogether, and they indicate that it is on the whole the more earthy part of their mind which can talk to us, and the newly developed part which remains outside. When it comes to controls like Phinuit and Feda, who are anonymous in the sense that there is no one alive who knew them on earth, it may be – we do not really know – that there is quite another part of Phinuit, quite another part of Feda, which gets left out, and perhaps has to get left out of the communication, just as Barrett and Drayton Thomas tell us that something of themselves has to stay outside.

In the same way therefore it is impossible to say how much of the whole mind either of a personal or of a teaching guide reaches us, and how much has to be left out due to our limitations of consciousness. If it is hard to discover in any full way what experiences even our near relatives have really undergone, how far their minds have travelled since what is after all a very recent death, we cannot hope to plumb the

* *When We Wake* (Collyer and Dampier), p. 212.

depths of a mind which may have had thousands of years in which to explore reality since its days on earth.

A guide demonstrates a detachment which suggests that he has cast off many limitations of temperament. How can we say whether fifty or one hundred or two thousand years may be needed to achieve this? After all, one earth life normally suffices for very little real spiritual growth. To expect an English professional man rapidly to become qualified as a guide involves a set of assumptions just as much as to accept a guide as an ancient being involves a different set.

Leaving assumptions and turning to evidence, how nearly has any posthumous English professional man come to being a guide? Perhaps the most favourable example is Myers, if indeed it is he who produced *The Road to Immortality*. In this book we cannot fail to perceive the *provisional* nature of the knowledge demonstrated. The posthumous Myers indeed insists on its being such. The mind behind it lacks the simplicity, the certainty and the authority which are to be found in some very humble guides who appear under a Red Indian guise, real or symbolic. There can be no doubt, to those who have had the experience of working with such guides, of the inferiority of the posthumous and still intellectual Myers. Again, in the records, at least as published, Myers gives no personal and individual guidance, although he certainly chides his mediums impatiently for their inabilities to receive his thoughts to his satisfaction. Again the inferiority is clear.

Although it is unwise to draw positive conclusions, there is little evidence to support any proposition that an English professional man in a generation or two has shown himself able to become a spiritual guide.

On the other hand, if an investigator is able to find a guide whose medium has been willing to undergo an earnest and dedicated discipline of mind and character in order to fulfil that guide's purpose, and if he then enters into a serious relationship of pupil and teacher with him, this can be made a highly practical demonstration of the guide's wisdom. For the investigator can see whether it brings about in time a steady deepening in his own character. He can also find out for himself whether he is able to discover the limits of the guide's mind. The ultimate core of significance in mediumistic communications lies far less in personal evidence, very necessary though this is in the first place, and far more in a joint effort to express on earth values put forward by guides, which will then demonstrate in action how far they prove valid.

11

In the modern world, less and less room seems to exist for the concept of an older spiritual brother, counsellor and friend. The modern man of intellect either relies upon technical experts, or else upon judging everything for himself; he usually does not find it an acceptable idea that there may exist even among living men an order of spiritual seniority.

If he ignores the concept that some ordinary modern men may be his elders in consciousness, whatever their earth age (as Shelley claimed to be older than his father), it is harder still to conceive of a being of superior wisdom in the person of a discarnate guide, who wishes to approach him and who expresses interest in him. Therefore, if in his sceptical way he comes into contact with such a guide, he is likely to be quite unattuned to such a relationship, and to pay little attention to the essential purpose of this variant of an immensely long religious tradition. The teacher-pupil, guru-chela, master-disciple relationship is the classic method of bringing about a change of consciousness. It is on this process, and not on dogma, that many of the true disciplines of religion have ultimately been based.

Discarnate guides clearly wish to restore this very ancient, well-tried tradition. Because it represents an individual process it might well appeal to a modern man, but what he often baulks at is that it needs another individual besides himself, namely the teacher, to complete it. He wishes instead to be his own moral teacher. To yield up authority to a guide is one thing, which intellectual integrity may wish to resist, but to refuse to listen to a guide as a possible moral teacher is another. If he does refuse this, then the relationship offered by the guide cannot be fulfilled.

When a reader of indisputed intellectual calibre takes up a book of mediumistic "wisdom", it is important for him to ask whether – behind all its faults and limitations of presentation – it contains anything which is beyond his present spiritual comprehension. This is not a palatable question, but it is a just one. If he asks himself: "Do I already understand it all perfectly clearly?" he is likely to answer affirmatively, but his criterion is an intellectual one and needs to be replaced by a different one, in terms of practical performance. In order to be correctly assessed, the teachings have first to be acte dout. And that is what the intellectual critic of them is very seldom prepared to do; he does not see any point in it.

> When we come into contact with you ... we find it almost impossible to bring through the grand truth that we have seen in the world of spirit. It is like trying to pour a great volume of liquid through a very small funnel. You see, what we have to say does not bring with it proof which the ... mind accepts. The only proof of these spiritual truths is that by (your) way of life you receive the proof and the demonstration of truth. To put it in very simple language: it *works* ... You can all prove it for yourselves but we cannot prove it for you; and any living man or woman can prove it if they like to apply the law to their daily lives.*

In one sense a guide says little that is new, since his words generally prove to be an expression of the teachings known as the Ancient Wisdom. Much, though by no means all, of what he says could have been found and pondered upon by the recipient for himself in one or other of the world's scriptures. The point is that the recipient has not found it, or if he has found it, has not made it bear any particular significance in his own life. The guide's task is to find a way for it into his pupil's heart, past the particular difficulties which bar its entry. Hence the combination of general teaching allied with particular insight into the individual pupil.

Thus the standard criticism made by intellectuals that entranced mediums only talk the "usual ethical twaddle" can be appropriate in two ways. It can be appropriate, of course, when the talk is, as it can be, no more than the unorganised outpourings of the medium's own mind, and is readily detected as such because the "control" lacks, when questioned, any specific insight into the individual spiritual problems of the unfortunate listeners. It can also be appropriate if the critic means either that he considers all ethical teaching is twaddle, or else, as he more probably does, that he thinks it is twaddle when it says no more than has already been said countless times before. He rejects it because it is moral advice in which he sees nothing new. It is not its content, but the familiarity or supposed familiarity of this content which makes him dismiss it as twaddle. Whether it is really twaddle depends upon the quality of the guide's insight, whether he puts his finger on something which the pupil, however clearly he thinks he knows it, is not practising. If a guide shows specific and purposeful insight into the individual, he is achieving something more difficult than being platitudinous. Unfortunately examples are practically impossible to give, since the nature of the process requires that the individual shall prove or disprove it for himself.

* *Student Teaching by White Eagle*, No. 173.

From one angle, the fact that a guide teaches what essentially is found in the world's scriptures is itself immensely heartening, especially since guides are invariably unwilling to bind themselves to any one creedal presentation. It is a confirmation – provided, of course, that the guide is really the ancient being he claims to be – of the reality of the insight which first produced these scriptures.

In general a guide attempts to accelerate the rate of growth of his pupil's consciousness beyond the normal pace at which it would be likely to grow through the ordinary experiences of life. Essentially of course the pupil has to find his own way; what the guide offers are certain aids by which he can re-orientate himself.

If guides are such wise beings, why should they trouble with anything so small as the increase of one man's insight into himself? No guide will ever overlook any person brought to him. The unit of spiritual progress is, and always has been, the individual.

> The principle on which we work is effecting lodgments, one at a time, no mass-conversion, no emotional evangelism, no hysterical appeals to salvation. The principle is to reach one at a time, one individual to be convinced through evidence, through logic, through understanding, through awakening, and then that individual, having made his link, to start his own attainment and unfoldment, and to fulfil the purpose of his life. This knowledge once attained, cannot be lost.*

* "Silver Birch"—*Two Worlds*, Jan. 1963, p. 83.

CHAPTER ELEVEN

Search and Research

I

How FAR is all this mediumistic communication what it purports to be? How far is the practical experience of the survivalist, with his different approach, in alignment with the ideas developed in the theories of psychical research? In the elements of that composite experience which makes up a sitting, how much supports and how much throws doubt upon apparent communication with discarnate beings? We are face to face with a central problem – the sources from which mediumistic material springs, or is drawn.

All experienced sitters agree, on either account of the facts, that the mind of a medium has a mirror-like quality. Most would agree that this mirror can turn itself in both directions, towards the sitter as well as towards the ostensible communicator. This power of reflection can bring acute difficulties for the observer, added to by the medium's own inability at times to know whence she draws the materials she reflects.

A past member of the Council of the S.P.R., once acting as chairman at an open meeting for the display of clairvoyance, found that the medium reproduced, to a member of the audience, and as a discarnate message, facts which the chairman had himself first become acquainted with on that very day, and which related to a different and living person. Who would dispute, if telepathy is accepted, that this is an example of telepathy from the living? The medium failed to recognise its source. Far from selecting her material, there is every indication that she was only reflecting it. Little in survivalist experience suggests that mediums can perform the feats which the theory of extended telepathy requires them to perform, the essence of which is instant and far-reaching selectivity, from any incarnate source, of just those facts which could have been in the memory of the discarnate person whom the medium claims is producing them. To reflect, without necessarily knowing either the accuracy or the source of what is reflected, coupled with a comparative inability to select – that is much closer to practical mediumistic performance.

There is of course an entirely different pattern of selection which is often observed, the mere habit of some platform mediums in obviously mentally asking each communicator in turn for the same kind of information – for instance, his age at death, his looks, his clothes, the names of his relatives. Such question-putting, which produces a stereotyped form of "message", is a sound indication that the medium is a second-rate one.

Experienced survivalists are well aware of the danger that matter which is in the mind of the sitter can be reflected back to him by the medium. This is more likely to happen when the sitter chooses to invade the delicate areas of the medium's receptivity with his own strongly-held emotions or emotionally-tinged beliefs. A sitter then readily but quite falsely comes to believe he has obtained discarnate confirmation of his particular prejudices. This happens the more easily if the medium's remarks happen to be combined with a correct description of hidden characteristics in the sitter, or facts from his past life. This information is not necessarily presented as of discarnate origin, but too many sitters assume that it must be, because they do not trouble to consider how the medium could otherwise have obtained it.

A sitter who is in serious doubt between two possible future courses of action open to him may find, although he has not disclosed his dilemma, that one medium will spontaneously suggest one of these courses, and a second medium the other. Each medium is almost certainly doing no more than reflecting back one part of the sitter's mind. More sensitive mediums, or perhaps the same medium on a different occasion, will successfully steer clear of such impingement from her sitters.

Confusion arises also through the communicator commencing one theme which at a later stage the medium turns into another one of her own, without recognising her own contribution.

As the Myers-Cummins figure writes:

> I wish to assure you that all my old friends who search so industriously for proofs of survival have an entire misconception as to the manner of communication and as to our attempts at controlling the medium. We do not control them, to a large extent they control us when we speak... It may seem strange to men and women that a revelation of our condition seldom comes through with clearness. That is the fault of the instrument which

cannot render the tune we would gladly play upon it. You must remember that a medium is rarely a mere medium. He should be called an "interpreter". It is an interpretation, not a literal statement, that is conveyed to you through him.*

Against the researcher's theory that mediums can by extended telepathy select almost at will, we have the constant complaint of discarnate communicators of something entirely different, that the medium fails to pick up their messages, or else distorts them. The posthumous Myers speaks of the intense loneliness of the communicator, throwing thoughts to the medium in vain, most of which will go unheeded. "I am a sensible woman," said one communicator to the writer. "What you hear is six-tenths me, and four-tenths the medium."

Once the productions of mediumship are seen by experience to suggest that they can be a compound product, many difficulties fall into place. A medium too can resemble a wireless set of poor selectivity, with interference from a second communicator overlapping with the intended one. The medium cannot separate out the different strands. A sitting is often an amalgam, where thoughts and feelings of medium, sitter and communicator (or more than one) float together, now the one coming into prominence, now the other, blending into a communication which does not wholly represent any one of them – the "no man's land" found by Drayton Thomas's communicator.

It is of course for the medium to bring into this delicate constantly shifting and interwoven field a principle of order, so that the stage can be held open as completely as possible for the main communicator. That is why it is so important that the sitter does not interfere too much with questionings and importunings, except when invited, for these are likely to touch off associations from elsewhere in the medium's mind, thus impinging upon, distorting and adding falsely to the image which the communicator, within the narrow limits available to him, is trying to project.

As John Drayton Thomas said to his son: "It would not be wise to rub canvas upon paints, it has to be done the other way round."†

2

The problem of mediumistic reflection of the sitter's hidden mind is the more complicated because it has a positive side. To the experienced

* *The Road to Immortality* (Geraldine Cummins), p. 182.
† *Proc.*, Vol. 38, p. 91.

sitter there is much to suggest that these two sources of material, the discarnate and the incarnate, frequently interpenetrate one another. Psychical research, as we have seen, is very rightly hypersensitive to the possibility of telepathy from the living masquerading in the medium's mind as discarnate material, to the medium failing to recognise the true source of her material, and dressing it up in a way appropriate to discarnate sources, since she has conditioned herself to suppose that it always comes thence. Research conceives extended telepathy as a fact-gathering process, a magpie-like filching from a number of different minds. It sees it in terms of gathering facts, because facts form the stuff of the evidence which it can properly assess. Practical observation suggests a different kind of mediumistic telepathy with the living, one which is primarily no fact-seeking process, nor always a mistaken reflection of facts present in the minds of other living persons, but rather a process of close attunement with the sitter's own hidden thoughts and feelings. There is little doubt that when the medium uses this power of looking with insight into the being of the sitter, she is using, though in a different direction, precisely the same faculty with which she claims to obtain information from the discarnate. Both arise from her attuning herself in the same way with another mind than her own. She has to achieve an extension of consciousness which French researchers very aptly term *lucidity*, and which leaves the question open whether the source of insight is incarnate or discarnate, or both.

It is strange, but when mediumship is working well these two insights – into the mind of the sitter and into the minds of the dead – often seem able to link themselves together with surprisingly little confusion. To the researcher this of course provides a strong suggestion that all mediumship is drawn from living sources: but to say that because some mediumistic information is undoubtedly drawn by telepathy from the living, it is possible for all of it to be so, differs entirely, of course, from bringing positive evidence that all of it is in fact so derived.

Experience thus suggests that lucidity into the mind of the sitter and into the discarnate mind cannot really be separated sharply off from one another on all occasions. It is the usual practice of a medium when she feels in direct touch with a discarnate source to endeavour to "tune out" the personality of the sitter before her. But if this direct touch does not come about, then some mediums endeavour to encourage it by focussing in the first place upon the sitter's inner self, until they "take off" into their proper realm. They perform a kind of pump-priming operation. By first becoming aware of something of the sitter's inner problems, they feel *thereby* enabled to become attuned in turn to discarnate communicators who wish to deal with these problems. Where their own telepathic insight or lucidity ends and that of a communicator begins is a delicate matter; but this comes to matter the less as the communicator's own personal evidence becomes stronger. Undoubtedly this forms one mode of entry sought by mediums into the discarnate realm, as distinct from tuning-in directly to a discarnate communicator. They link into such a communicator by the route of the sitter's mind; intellectually tempting though it is to conclude that everything subsequently continues to be drawn thence, it is not necessarily so.

There are of course occasions when the medium does not find the lift she requires; then sittings can degenerate into a wretched exhibition of mediumistic patter, a desperate casting-around in the hope that sooner or later a chord will be struck which will result in the stimulation of her genuine faculty. A blank sitting usually demonstrates all too well this casting-around process. Even worse is the fourth-rate professional medium who makes a habit of general statements of a kind which are likely to apply to the majority of her sitters.

3

Practical experience of trance controls leads to the problem whether their source lies only in the deeper subliminal parts of the medium's own mind, those which in dreams express themselves in images of archetypal form from the collective unconscious. Some guides, for instance, play a role suggestively similar to the figure of the old wise man of Jungian analysis. The whole gallery of figures which appear in the mediumistic trance, and which so often resemble similar figures in the trance-state of other mediums, it could be said, represent no more than psychic fragments of the medium's self, which come to the fore through dissocation by the medium from her normal daily self.

Feda could be dismissed as a mere dramatic presentation of the garnering powers possessed by the medium's unconscious mind, once it becomes dissociated from the cares and responsibilities which weigh down and ballast the conscious daily mind, and can therefore be appropriately represented by a childish figure. On the other hand it would then be likely that familiarity with Feda over the years would show her up as a simulacrum, but experience shows that her vividness remains unimpaired, even to conscious and critical observers.

Perhaps the problem lies less in the machinery than in discovering its real operator; if these presentations can be traced back to the medium's own being, it can still be that discarnate personages are really at work behind them, who can only appear to the sitter as a result of laying hold, in whatever imperfect way they can, of the psychological machinery which already exists for them to manipulate within the medium's make-up. Ambrose Pratt, writing posthumously to his friend Professor Raynor Johnson through the medium Geraldine Cummins, states that her control, Astor, "is both a secondary personality of Miss Cummins, and an individual who once lived on earth."*

Some process of strengthening and animating these potential figures in the medium's psyche may be the only method to break through and gain access to the sitters at all.

Some psychologists may perfectly correctly relate a Feda-type of child-figure to subconscious aspects and a teaching guide to super-conscious' aspects of the medium's personality. Again, discarnate communication is not necessarily absent. The figures of child and of guide may be necessary factors which serve to hold the medium's psyche together, as it were, and canalise the perhaps powerful thoughts of discarnate beings through aspects of the medium which she can again absorb safely into herself when the trance is over, and which form essential factors in both bringing about the trance and in preserving the medium from possible ill-effects of it. In other words, discarnate possession perhaps takes effect in hidden parts of the personality; what we see in these figures is largely the outer machinery. Once the machinery is well established, the medium is likely at times to be convinced that the guide is at work, when really no more than her own unconscious self is operating the machinery; at other times some sort of blending of the two is to be expected. A medium may need protective psychic apparatus of some sort to secure herself against continuous or disorderly invasion, not necessarily only from discarnate sources. Disrupting invading communications, whether from the medium's own unconscious, or from outside sources making use of it, are common enough in spiritualistic experience, probably commoner indeed than are medically

* *The Light and the Gate* (Raynor Johnson), p. 141.

observed secondary personalites in cases like Sally Beauchamp and Eve of the Three Faces. The breaking-up or invasion of the psyche has to be guarded against. Pragmatic experience of survivalists warns every tyro that defences are very necessary to a medium against weaknesses both of sensibility and of character, which can make her a victim of invasion which she cannot resist.

When Drayton Thomas's discarnate relatives accept Feda as an independent being, as they imply that they do when they talk to the sitter, the question has to be posed whether she is only treated as separate because they themselves in turn are no more than figures simulated in their absence by the medium's dramatising mind, although the information they give and even the sentiments they express are so appropriate to the real beings represented.

Now experience suggests that figures of dead people are represented at times by the medium's own control.

> ... in a sitting of Dr. Thaw's, when his friend Dr. H. was supposed to be communicating, not directly, but through Phinuit, a long speech was made so characteristic of Dr. H. that Dr. Thaw, wishing to know whether he or Phinuit was speaking, said, "Can you tell me anything about Dr. Phinuit?" The answer was, "I'm talking to you myself, you rascal; I'm talking for him." "Well," said Dr. Thaw, "you're trying to make us think he's talking," to which Phinuit replied, "I'm simply telling you what he says. I'm trying to imitate him."*

The Myers figure who is claimed as writing through Geraldine Cummins states that he can build up a likeness of himself, and

> ... send that likeness speeding across our vast world to a friend, to one, that is, in tune with me. Instantly I appear before that friend though I am remote from him; and my likeness holds speech – in thought, remember, not words – with this friend. Yet, all the time, I control it from an enormous distance; and as soon as the interview is concluded I withdraw the life of my thought from that image of myself, and it vanishes.†

Whether Phinuit is a real being or only a figure built up in Mrs. Piper's mind, it may be that he (or she) often "presents" a real communicator, even if the representation has its faults and incompletenesses. Not every communicator may be skilled enough in thought-control to present it for himself, as Myers claims he can do. Seen in this light, the Dr. H. - Phinuit presentation perhaps earns more credit than

---

* *Proc.*, Vol. 13, p. 567.
† *The Road to Immortality* (Geraldine Cummins), pp. 60–1.

Phinuit was ever able to earn for himself alone. Such a process might explain why some controls get into a muddle when cross-examined by the sitter, or even fail to answer easy questions.

Most experienced sitters suspect, indeed, that at times an element of stage management is at work, and that things are not necessarily quite as they are represented as being. But, again, who does the stage managing – some aspect of the medium, bent on deceit, or a discarnate communicator?

It still remains hard for an experienced and successful sitter to dismiss the likelihood that, on stage or off stage, discarnate communicators exist, and that essentially the communications frequently have their ultimate source in them. Although the focus is often so imperfect, communicators do present themselves at times in a close and convincing manner, and sustain their hold upon the medium in a consistent way. The sense of their presence then becomes very strong. It is appearances of this kind which carry the survivalist over the more fragmentary and baffling appearances discussed above.

In examining these mediumistic utterances, the psychologist of course is likely to emphasise the dramatising unconscious elements in them, as the psychical researcher is likely to draw out their ESP elements, and the survivalist their communicator elements; each element may be present; all may be observing correctly.

As we have previously seen, there are in a reasonably vivid sitting a number of factors which only the sitter's subjective judgment can sum up; the presentation of character, nuances of relationship, remarks which though brief irresistibly suggest the communicator claimed. The Rev. Bayfield* found indications in the Statius script of the very tones of the voice of his old friend Doctor Verrall. More often, however, much which gave a sitting its vividness is found, when subsequently put down on paper, to have evaporated, even for the sitter. Good sittings, as has been said, are characterised by a sense of presence, which is most hard to describe. Even a tape recorder cannot reproduce all of this experience. That is why some sitters put more faith in their scepticism than in their own memories, and gradually come to doubt whether their original impressions ever occurred.

To decide whether material is more likely to be of incarnate or discarnate origin requires many specific and individual acts of judgment, acts which the survivalist and the researcher alike sometimes refuse to

* Page 68, above.

make, because each holds that all is from one kind of source only. The experienced sitter tries to find out ways to judge which are based on growing familiarity with mediumistic productions at first hand; he may take as many years to make up his mind as did Sir Oliver Lodge and Mrs. Sidgwick. He will certainly keep an area in which to set many statements which must remain for the time being not proven, and which only subsequent experience can verify. First-hand observation of mediumship requires factors of judgment, as we have seen, which cannot all be set down in the comments possible in a paper record.

A characteristic of mediumistic communications is that they are best helped by providing opportunity for the good material to be subsequently enlarged upon, and for the irrelevant to drop away. Like Theseus, the recipient has to pursue his Ariadne thread past many false passages. The threads received by the medium sometimes arrive in a tangled ball; it is sometimes better for the sitter to take hold of the thread related to him; by his response, the thread may be drawn more certainly forth by the medium, who then gains confidence that she is on the right track. There is of course a great difference between helping the communicator along, and merely helping the evidence along, and still more between offering facts for the medium subsequently to pass back to the sitter. It is in terms of a human relationship that both medium and communicator require the recipient's help. Clearmindedness, resource and emotional stability in the sitter are valuable allies to the communicator. Communication after all is a form of impeded conversation. If the communication is not reciprocal, how can it be expected to yield its best? As is often said by survivalists, every sitting has to be regarded as an experiment and its outcome can never be forecast. It is an experiment, but an open one, which has to be allowed to some degree to take shape spontaneously; it is here that it differs from normal scientific experiments. The sitter is dealing with a situation where at best a discarnate communicator cannot obtain more than a foothold, and a temporary foothold at that, in the consciousness of the medium. It can only be misleading to expect that the material must represent the full consciousness and memory of the communicator, when there is every appearance that it is often nothing of the kind, but a product of limitations which the more analytical communicators themselves describe and state that they cannot wholly overcome.

In a recent German mining disaster, after some survivors had been brought to the surface, possible indications were heard of a second group of buried survivors, but of so faint and uncertain a kind as to make their existence extremely unlikely. Nevertheless the issue was far too important to ignore the slightest possible indication of the presence of living men. The indications were followed up, and the men were found and rescued. The analogy may apply to discarnate survivors, who are able to give indications, which though imperfect are far more forceful than the miners were able to produce.

4

It would be reasonable to expect that the fruits of direct, seasoned experience of communications, of careful assessment of the aspects which have to be weighed subjectively, and that the exposition of its moral and philosophical teachings could be looked for at their best in organised Spiritualism. But this is not so. Public opinion puts a low estimate on Spiritualism, and public opinion, though doubtless partly activated by irrelevant considerations, amongst them ignorance of the facts and fear of the unknown, is yet not far astray in this particular conclusion. Why is this? Spiritualism often seems to prefer its own worst to its own best. It has undoubtedly made a very poor use of its opportunities. Like many minorities, it suffers from extremely limited powers of self-criticism. As a movement, Spiritualism remains full of confusion because it has never really decided where it is going. The normal spiritualist church service combines a form of worship, a demonstration of evidence, and an act of entertainment. The medium is expected to perform these varied rites together, which is nearly impossible. Some Spiritualists consider it a religion. Others claim that it is "scientific", by which they usually mean that it is based on observable experience, however uncritical the observation. Others try to make out of it a philosophy of living, freed from all religious dogma; in Spiritualists this readily falls into a refusal to follow the inferences of their own thought as soon as it passes beyond a simple moral code and begins to lead on towards the classical problems of religion and philosophy.

By the comfortable personal acceptance of messages, of which all the edges are blurred into indefiniteness, by preferring the shallow message because it is less demanding than a serious one, by the reporting of messages with their ambiguities glossed over, by injudicious praise of mediums in the interests of propaganda – in a word, by the complete absence of that search for perfection by which the great human activities have always been nourished, Spiritualists, by these lax standards, encourage their mediums to believe they are more skilled than they really are in their difficult task, and thus at present ensure a continuing mediocrity.

Just as a number of compulsive sceptics find their way by a process of natural attraction to psychical research, so Spiritualism is plagued in turn by compulsive fantasy-hunters. In the magic-working drama which Spiritualism sometimes seems to offer them in place of a drab ineffectuality in ordinary life, there is plenty to nourish illusion.

If, too, discarnate communication is accepted, inevitably a tendency arises to bestow upon it an authority, quite other than it may wish to claim for itself. Myth-making man all too readily and too lazily declares that material which he believes to be of discarnate origin is *thereby* of superior authority to his own, and therefore prima facie to be accepted. Even if errors, imperfections and interruptions in the process of transmission are accepted – and we have seen that nobody could deny them – there is the problem of status: one's grandfather and one's guide may have access to very different levels of consciousness. Over and over again, guide communicators insist that there shall be accepted from them only what the recipient's own consciousness endorses from within. Yet, once discarnate communication is accepted, it is undoubtedly difficult at times to escape imposing an authority upon communicators of a kind which can easily get out of hand. The assumption that if a message has a discarnate source, then the advice it gives must be good, is a non sequitur into which Spiritualists often fall. Whether the advice is good or bad is of course an issue separate altogether from whether its source is discarnate or not.

It is interesting to note the warnings given through Spiritualism's own communicators. Here are posthumous words purported to be from Arthur Conan Doyle, the acknowledged leader of Spiritualism whilst he was alive.

> Before my passing I had little understanding of the many difficulties holding up communication with the spirit world, but I became convinced of the reality of that communication on cold evidence – which I now recognise might not have been so valid as I once thought... The Spiritualist ... has yet far to go and will find many snares, pitfalls, and illusions in his contacts with the astral. Psychic or magnetic forces which surround the human environment are often responsible for phenomena which are too readily accepted as evidence of communication from a spirit. Much can be

found in the sitter's own mentality and magnetism to account for these; and then also there are deceiving spirits which find their amusement in the impersonation of well-known personalities. This I have myself witnessed with some disquiet . . . This lack of intelligence and vitality can be found throughout the phenomena of Spiritualism – in manifestations by means of ouija boards or materialisation, or the direct voice. These phenomena are comparable to bubbles; prick them, and if they lack a sustaining intelligence, they fall to nothing. Investigate this for yourselves by your observation . . . I do not wish for one moment to belittle the value of all spiritualistic phenomena. Undoubtedly there are genuine manifestations. But there still remains much which is merely shadowy . . . The crux of the whole matter depends on the quality of the mind or the purity of the aspirations of the person who would communicate with a spirit. If a human mind is attuned to . . . love and service a perfectly intelligent communication will be the result; but if a man's mind be only nebulous, untrained and lacking in spiritual understanding, trouble of some sort will be the outcome . . . All these phenomena, all this continual running to mediums by people who want to keep in continual touch with the dead, is wrong. Men must seek rather for the living Light of Truth . . . which knowledge of the laws governing human survival may help them to understand. Only with this object in view should men seek to lift the veil between the two worlds.*

There is a further and opposite difficulty which arises when the communicator does attempt to speak from his present self, and of his present conditions. Again it is a difficulty to which far too little attention is given by Spiritualists. This difficulty is that the newly arrived communicator may himself be unconscious of his own limitations and lack of understanding of his new life; the information he gives may be ill-founded.

A communicator is describing his experiences soon after death.

He told me he was a messenger from another sphere, higher up . . . "You are speaking to earth. Do not hurry to describe your new life and surroundings. Take my advice; do a little living first." I think he saw surprise in my face. "Do you know," he continued, "that most of what you have conveyed to your friend at the matter end of the line is quite illusory?" "What do you mean?" I cried. "You will gradually find out for yourself. Remember what I have said." This conversation has perturbed me. I try to dismiss it from my mind, but it sticks. It makes me feel smaller still. Am I really the fool rushing in where angels fear to tread? After all what do I know about my present life?†

Again, from the posthumous Arthur Conan Doyle:

What (communicators) pass on is more or less their own personal opinion

* *The Return of Arthur Conan Doyle* (Ivan Cooke), pp. 74–80.
† *Private Dowding* (Anon.), p. 31.

... we find that many controls in spiritualistic circles set out only their own viewpoint and outline their own ideas. For he who dwells in the astral spheres narrows down his experience of the after-life, much as a man on earth clings to fixed opinions, political or religious. Maybe he thinks that he possesses the whole truth, and that his convictions are final. Every soul, however – and this is important – must eventually walk that path whereon he becomes *cleansed from all assertion.**

These warnings have largely fallen on wilfully deaf ears. There are of course within Spiritualism sincere people, practical in outlook and intention, well endowed with common sense and of ample worldly experience, who regularly apply themselves to the spiritualistic task of comforting the mourner, of practising control of thought, and of giving weight to the true motives which lie behind their own actions. These deplore the superficialities and ineffectualities they find in organised Spiritualism, but they have so far failed to alter it.

Nevertheless Spiritualists at times receive sharp and vivid experiences. It is this impact of direct experience upon which the Spiritualist takes his stand. Sometimes the evidence speaks so vividly that unfortunately it seems pointless to him to record it in the orderly way required by researchers. Those who have an ear for human testimony often sense in these imperfect accounts an underlying validity, even though, like most reminiscences, they can become improved with repetition and by memory's selective aid. Careful Spiritualists come to know the reliable witnesses amongst themselves; their own experience helps in assessing that of others. But all these remain particular and largely private experiences.

5

Mediumship in public is carried on under conditions necessarily unfavourable to it. It has to be accepted that the best and most delicate and most sustained mediumship is that carried on in private. There are two quite different Spiritualisms, the public and the private. Private working groups form the real spearhead of Spiritualism. These are normally closed groups, entered only by invitation. They are very seldom opened to the odd visitor, and never to the beginner or casual enquirer. For casual membership destroys the conditions essential for this work. Such a group compares with most public church mediumship as a lieder recital with a village concert. Only by unification of

* *The Return of Arthur Conan Doyle*, p. 76.

purpose can the very delicately balanced psychic conditions be built up in which trance teaching can be given consistently at its best, and in which active spiritual work can be undertaken by a group. This work is always concerned in one way or another with service of an outward-going kind, and with the gradual refining and changing of the individual consciousness. Its members have to be prepared to work for a considerable while without any tangible results. It has no publicity value, nothing to talk about. It never involves trying to produce unusual psychic phenomena, or the gaining and wielding of any personal power. It works as a group. It is as harmless as a group of monks or nuns entering their chapel in order to pray, and indeed rather resembles such groups.

It recalls the immemorial eastern method of teaching; the trance teacher is the guru, the group are his chelas, with the difference that the guru is no longer on earth.

The number of these groups, quietly carrying on their work from year to year, is almost certainly small. Whenever Spiritualism reaches towards its best, however, such groups become formed.

The most embarrassing question which a newcomer can ask of a Spiritualist is: "Where can I find good mediumship?" For the correct answer at present is: "In very few places." The most difficult question he can ask is this: "If these teaching guides are such elevated beings, why is public Spiritualism so unimpressive?" The answer is short: its working committees take no notice from one year's end to the other of what guides teach; they are the last sources they will ever consult.

The average Spiritualist wants his Spiritualism at a bargain price, but in any exploration of reality there are no bargains to be found.

It is not in popular Spiritualism that the critical enquirer will find his way into the heart of the matter.

6

It is greatly to be regretted that further exploration of the qualitative field has for so many years been left to survivalists who are often intellectually or technically unsophisticated in exploring it. Psychical research, by its lack of interest in the communication aspects of mediumship during the last thirty years, must accept some of the blame for the fact that mediumistic standards of evidence have become low. It has done virtually nothing to encourage mediums to work to its own standards, as earlier workers for instance so successfully encouraged and supported Mrs. Leonard to do.

It is a thousand pities that the two approaches have been so widely separated, when so much more might have been achieved had they won a mutual respect from one another.

An illustration may show just how cerebral psychical research has become in its approach.

> A woman whom I had met a few times . . . and liked, was killed in an aeroplane accident. Two days later I seemed acutely aware of her presence, and she implored me to stop a course of action which was being taken by a close relative for her sake . . . I thought the action most improbable . . . The situation was as I had been told and I was able to put it right.
>
> "Did you see the woman?" asked the investigator when I reported this experience. "No." "Did you hear what she said?" "No." "Then how did you know she was there?" "I didn't *know*. But it felt like her – her personality." "I see. And if you didn't hear what she said, how did you know what it was?" "I can't explain. She seemed to communicate it inside me . . . We seemed to be in – in communion." The investigator looked pained . . . "You realise," he said, "that there is no evidence here at all." "No, of course not," I said meekly, thinking of the intensity of the experience. "I suppose," he said, "that you are firmly convinced of survival?" "No," I replied, "I've never been able to envisage it." . . . It is very tempting to dismiss (these cases) as spurious because their assumed interpretation seems improbable. Nevertheless they remain facts of experience.*

It is very clear that some investigators, like the one encountered by this unfortunate percipient, are completely ignorant of what an ESP experience is really like. It is after all an experience they have never had. Unfortunately some are unwilling to make up for this defect by making a serious attempt to understand as far as possible what it is like through the eyes of a sensitive.

A member of the S.P.R. has recorded an extremely interesting experience of his own.

> . . . I found myself in a peculiarly tranquil and peaceful frame of mind, which I cannot easily describe. (I think now that this was really the initial stage of the experience itself and was brought about by some exterior influence) . . . in a gentle and gradual way, it began to dawn on me that there was someone else in the room, located fairly precisely about two yards away, to my right front. It was the experience which some psychical researchers call "the sense of presence". There was no sensory hallucination at all . . . I neither saw my "visitor" nor heard him, though I was quite sure

---

* *The Sixth Sense* (Rosalind Heywood), p. 177.

about his presence and his location. (Why then did I think of him as male? I don't know. All I can say is that it seemed obvious.) The experience was not in the least alarming. On the contrary it was a very delightful one. I liked my "visitor" very much.

Then we proceeded to have a conversation, conducted entirely by exchange of thoughts; there was still no sort of sensory hallucination. It was on a theological subject – the love of God for human beings. In the course of this conversation, my "visitor" showed an intimate knowledge of my most private thoughts and feelings, and I got a strong impression of his personality. He seemed to me very good and very wise and most kindly disposed towards me. I liked and respected him greatly. I am sure I have never had a more welcome visitor.

... gradually I passed from exchanging thoughts with my visitor into a private meditation or rumination on what he had said. And after a while, I became aware that he was no longer there. But the effects of his "visit" lasted for the whole of that day, and they have not altogether ceased even yet. They altered my whole attitude to religion ...

To apply a reductive criticism to such accounts is one discipline, and a necessary one. To assess them as experiences which are positive in content requires a different discipline which also is needed in order to try to determine gradually whether or not the sense of presence in them – which the subject in this case described as "not just the presence of 'someone or other' but of a person with a very distinct individuality" – can have its source in some being other than the subject, or only in some part of himself which is somehow exteriorised in his perception. It is important to try and compare impressions where the sense of presence points towards an individual who cannot be identified in name, as in this case, with other impressions which, even if derived through different techniques, point, as the Rev. Bayfield found the Statius script did, to a particular deceased person who had been very familiar to him when alive. To do so we need the help of the participant in as many cases as possible, but at present if he moves in highly educated circles, however interesting he finds such happenings in other people, he is often unwilling to make his own similar experiences known.

Dr. Gilbert Murray thus described his experiences of telepathy:

The conditions which suited me best were in many ways much the same as those which professional mediums have sometimes insisted upon. This is suspicious, yet fraud, I think, is out of the question ... I liked the general atmosphere to be friendly and familiar; any feeling of ill-temper or hostility was apt to spoil an experiment. Noises or interruption had a bad effect ... At one time, indeed, I was inclined to attribute the whole thing to subconscious auditory hyperaesthesia . . . but . . . there were some clear cases where I got a point or even a whole subject which had only been thought and not spoken.

Of course, the personal impression of the percipient himself is by no means conclusive evidence, but I do feel there is one almost universal quality in these guesses of mine which does suit telepathy and does not suit any other explanation. They always begin with a vague emotional quality or atmosphere . . . That seems like a direct impression of some human mind. Even in the failures this feeling of atmosphere often gets through. That is, it was not so much an act of cognition, or a piece of information that was transferred to me, but rather a feeling or an emotion; and it is notable that I never had any success in guessing mere cards or numbers, or any subject that was not in some way interesting or amusing.*

Professor Murray considered it necessary to apologise for feeling in the way a medium says she does. This mental climate of our time results in the suppression of what may be a considerable amount of private first-hand evidence of telepathic experience among intelligent people. Concerning this, there is a cultural conspiracy of silence. In intimate friendship, people will sometimes admit to such experiences but not when in professional and social company, for fear of adverse judgment which may silently be passed upon them, and might even prejudice their professional careers. After Professor Raynor Johnson had published *The Imprisoned Splendour*, many people wrote to him, describing psychic and mystical experiences of their own; when he subsequently published a selection of these it must have brought reassurance to others with similar experiences, possibly far outnumbering those who had been courageous enough to write.

ESP, as Professor Johnson's correspondents found as well as Professor Murray, involves often the transfer of emotion and thought, sometimes with an instantaneous precision beyond the power of words; sometimes it brings forth a state of consciousness never before known to the percipient. As many others besides Professor Murray have found, Zener cards are singularly ill-fitted for all that telepathy at its most characteristic can achieve; Zener cards are used as a measuring device, but all but the narrowest subject-matter of telepathy can perhaps never be measured at all.

These experiences need to be dealt with by other ways than those of organised Spiritualism, with its naïve pictures of undoubtedly complex phenomena, and its self-satisfaction in rating as conclusive evidence a

* *Proc.*, Vol 49, p. 162.

great deal of material which is nothing of the kind. If these more intimate sorts of extra-sensory experiences were gradually to find acceptance at a better intellectual level, where they are at present, if fragmentary, often allowed to pass by practically unnoticed, or if noticed regarded as being of little value, they might gradually be recognised as occurring more often than is at present supposed. The more skilled and sensitive attention they could then receive might find in them subtle and significant human experiences, which in time might make their way into literature and song, and eventually be enriched by every kind of human insight playing upon them.

Telepathic impressions of this non-laboratory kind vary from fully conscious perceptions to a vague, barely conscious sense, perhaps of evil, or of a friendly presence. Its apparently spontaneous and unpredictable character must not mask that, like any other talent, it is likely to be improved by attention and practice. It seems best suited to the accurate transfer less of facts than of complex states of being which elude ready verbal expression. Discarnate communicators, if we choose to believe them, make use of telepathy because it surpasses the limits of verbal communication, and they say they do so not only when attempting to communicate with us on earth, but as a natural mode of expression between themselves. If the mental climate of our time gradually comes to regard telepathy as a refined form of communication of a socially acceptable kind, instead of as something that is better kept silent about because others will consider it an illusion or even as a form of mental illness, then it may be on the road to becoming a valued mode of communication, and the hopes expressed by Dr. Gilbert Murray in a presidential address to the S.P.R. be fulfilled.

> I believe most of us in this Society are inclined to agree with Bergson that ... (telepathy) ... is probably a common unnoticed phenomenon in ordinary life, especially between intimates. We all know how often two friends get the same thought at the same moment. Tolstoy, the most acute of observers, speaks of "the instinctive feeling with which one human being guesses another's thoughts, and which serves as the guiding thread of conversation." ... And what about the impression people receive from the shared enjoyment of drama, poetry, music, or even, I think, some of the more imaginative branches of philosophy? Is there not some telepathy, some shared sensitivity, at work – not very different from that which a dog feels when he shares the trouble or anxiety of his master? And shall I be wrong in suggesting that it is just in these cases that our main instrument, language, rather fails us and, like the dog, we have to appeal to something less perfectly articulate? ... I suspect that what we call genius is a special sensitiveness in this region of

art, poetry, thought and the like: a sensitiveness which according to many critics is apt to be deadened and disregarded by our all-absorbing material civilisation, and if so is disregarded at our peril ... it may well be that William James was right in his forecast that the work of this Society may ultimately render great service to the religious gropings of the human mind.*

The service which the S.P.R. can render, however, since it must spring from its own terms of reference, needs to be supplemented by witnesses, pursuing a parallel way in fields, sometimes within or very close to psychical research, at other times very far from from it.

When Mrs. Sidgwick, whose approach was as close as possible to that of strict psychical research, admitted into her private judgment more than research can allow, was she reading the evidence more completely, and also more rightly? Was she offering valuable help to others who, like her, face the problem of what witnesses from within their own being they will ultimately allow to influence their private verdict?

A modern poet has put the point with a whimsical clarity all his own. Walter de la Mare says:

> How much of one's experience is unverifiable! Take the Society for Psychical Research: what self-respecting ghost would co-operate in their tests?†

Some "ghosts", as the records show, have proved to be persistent and even to display a sense of evidence; others, provided we are careful, may come to be known more fully and perhaps ultimately more truly in other than our scientific witnessings, necessary though the latter will always remain.

A most notable ghost has now appeared, in the person of Mrs. Willett, in scripts through Geraldine Cummins which must surely create something of a watershed in the literature of psychical research. These began when her identity still remained a closely guarded secret known only to a small and eminently reticent group of researchers, but not to Miss Cummins. When by the evidence Miss Cummins herself began to guess the identity of her new communicator, she still did not know that the many direct facts of Mrs. Willett's life already given in the scripts were nearly all correct, as were subsequent ones, and of the few incorrect facts, the important ones – for instance that one of her sons went to Eton, not Winchester – were mostly corrected in later scripts.

* *Proc.*, Vol. 49, pp. 162-9.
† *Tea with Walter de la Mare* (Russell Brain), p. 23.

The bare facts, however, are only a secondary factor serving to support the primary factor, which is the fascinating self-painted character portrait of Mrs. Willett, subtle, complex and very positive, and which correctly refers to her work as a magistrate, as a delegate to the League of Nations in Geneva, and in the causes of Welsh art and nationalism. During the two and a quarter years over which the scripts arrived, the eagerness with which she set out to prove her identity to a son who disbelieved in survival changes later into an acceptance that since she has become convinced of their essential love for one another, his present beliefs now no longer really matter; to another son, in one of the final scripts, she brings a most moving confession of how in his very early years she felt she had created a barrier, first by a want of love, and then by an over-preponderant possessive love, and again later, because he refused this, by a turning away from him in hurt and annoyance, and she begs, for *her* sake now, for his forgiveness, and offers both her sons an equal love.

No fair-minded reader could ever say again that nothing but trivialities are communicated in mediumistic evidence. When, as here, scripts show the coming about over a period of time of vivid changes initiated by a communicator in her relationships with living persons, they strike a blow at the extended telepathy theory. These are a mother's feelings, not those of the sons to whom they are addressed, from whom by the extended telepathy theory the facts given would need to be drawn. The sceptic unable to accept Mrs. Willett is almost forced to say that these feelings, changing feelings at that, must have been invented by the automatist. Feelings, unfortunately, cannot be proved, in the same way as the facts from which they proceed; and in Mrs. Willett's case the feelings were clearly far more important than the facts. The Mrs. Willett of the scripts, as a changing, sentient being, surely shows herself, if one may say so, as someone eminently worthy of survival.

At the request, she states, of her old sitter, Gerald Balfour, now also dead, she withdraws her refusal to publish some of her own most precious mediumistic experiences, those in the Palm Sunday case, which relate to the young Arthur Balfour's tragic love story. And what of the Dark Young Man? In one of the earliest scripts, before Mrs. Willett's identity had been guessed, Astor, Miss Cummins's main communicator, writes of Francis. This was the real name of the Dark Young Man, who, it will be remembered, died on Mont Blanc.

... his life was cut short in some sport. There is an accident, a crash. He died from a fall, away in some foreign country. [She] is so pleased, so excited to meet him. "I wasn't mistaken," she says. "Of course we knew each other quite well."*

Astor is clearly puzzled, as he goes on to say:

> I don't quite understand the connection between these two. They met and talked on a number of occasions in some odd, unusual circumstances.†

The two of course never met in life, but only through Mrs. Willett's conscious perception of him through her own mediumship.

As one posthumous highly skilled medium working upon the equally though quite differently skilled living mind of another, Mrs. Willett's comments on some of the more subtle difficulties of communication are of extreme interest.

> When we converse through a medium ... we become, as it were, dependent on her thoughts, words and images, and we go wrong, we stray in that tide. It can be a River of Forgetfulness temporarily too, for the struggling communicator in many cases, and it can be a mixture; part the automatist, part the communicator, or it can come in flashes and be almost true. I say this for your encouragement, as I see how much you doubt and want to be done with it all. I know those moods. I had them at times. But what was always sure, true and wonderful to me were my other world visions, and these were not my imagination. I have since my passing rediscovered them, found they are what the S.P.R. call veridical!‡
>
> The subliminal mind of the automatist might be likened to the earth in which here and there are sown the seeds of real evidence. That subliminal produces many weeds that have to be discarded.§
>
> Occasionally her subliminal mind enters my mind, plunders an idea or memory. It is not all a one-way traffic.
>
> Then, of course, her mind may insert in patches its own mistaken interpretation. Supernal and infernal juggling can occur.‖

Worthy of the closest attention, too, are her comments on the cross-correspondences.

> The ... Case might be likened to an orchestra's perfect performance. The several communicators were scholars, whose intellects were married to imaginations that cherished an ideal image of scholarly perfection in the evidence ... The investigators and the mediums had sufficient imagination to envisage the ... objective of perfection. Thus deep called to deep in a unified desire. An orchestra must play as one if the performance is to reach towards perfection ...

* *Swan on a Black Sea* (Geraldine Cummins), p. 10.
† Ibid., p. 10.   ‡ Ibid., p. 25.
§ *Ibid.*, p. 105.   ‖ Ibid., p. 64.

> It is when imaginative desire fails on the part of human beings otherwise fitted for the work that "cases peter out" ... At the present time imagination is too completely subservient to the intellect among well-educated people. The overriding intellect produces sterility of imagination. Such people are therefore ... incompetent as investigators: they are bound, if they investigate, only to meet with negative results. But atheists or agnostics who do not subdue the imaginative desire of the explorer will, granted other conditions, a skilled medium, etc., obtain fruitful results.*
>
> If psychical research is to make progress, more attention should be paid to the selection of a qualified sitter ...
>
> An automatist can obtain interesting results – even striking ones – from making contact with an effective and qualified communicator. But for really impressive results maintained over a long period, a trio is needed – the third in the trio is the sitter.†
>
> The opposite to Gerald and O.L. [Oliver Lodge] is the egocentric sitter who has a deep-seated complex, such as a repressed horror of death, or inordinate vanity that derives from an insecurity fear. How dreadful to the egocentric is the thought that others might deem him credulous!‡

From all this it is very clear how Mrs. Willett, if it is she, calls from her new vantage-point for much more from the sitter than many a psychical researcher considers he needs to give: a desire to know, a kind of imaginative exploring passion. His caution, his disbelief, his scepticism, matter not at all, but what is essential is an openness to some degree of inner adventure. The formidable barrier of hostility in the present intellectual climate is one of the greatest enemies of exploration of the paranormal.

* *Swan on a Black Sea* (Geraldine Cummins), p. 58.
† Ibid., p. 106. ‡ Ibid., p. 105.

CHAPTER TWELVE

Summing-up

1

THE problem of survival, then, is as complex as it is momentous, for the various levels at which it can be approached criticise and contradict one another; they do not fall into place in a generally accepted hierarchy of values. The Eastern Orthodox Church conceives of truth in a way which it calls *soborny*, literally catholic, but possibly better translated as symphonic. The problem of survival can be regarded by a similar process, a symphonic weaving together of many differing and even seemingly contradictory contributions and perceptions, each with its own values and limitations. In this chapter let us attempt a small *sobornost*, a placing briefly side by side of some of these differing aspects.

2

There are many who consider it wiser to judge the possibility of survival from a different set of facts altogether than those which offer any direct evidence of it. They consider that life itself tells the answer and makes any apparent evidence of survival likely to be illusory; for from their knowledge of human nature they ask whether, after all, man is *worth* survival, and answer that he is not.

For if, they say, there is put aside the blind instinctive animal in us which fears to die, and stock is taken of what else is left, does very much remain which is worth the keeping? Are we so enamoured of this rest of us which the animal is struggling to preserve?

Viewed with detachment, much of what persists in a man forms a degrading and useless self-prison, a disjointed, unedifying and self-defeating jumble from which he himself, if he lives long enough, is content to escape. So is not his demise a good riddance? If he has become tired of himself in his seventy or eighty years, how could he go on tolerating such a self for an indefinite or even an infinite future? To those who are forced by their reading of experience to such a view, it seems an ignoble weakness to long for, or expect, survival.

If man is equated thus with the sum of his own diminishing attributes, successively attacked as they are by the onset of age, and with all the limitations which time brings, he becomes a mere wasting asset, which it is highly appropriate for death to write off. Better to rule the line sternly across the page for ever.

Again, survival can seem a wholly impossible notion if it means, as many communicators claim, that after death one becomes not only possessed of a somehow rejuvenated form, in place of this present self shrunken and withered by time, but restored in mind also to full vigour of consciousness. Does not this imply an impossible reversal? For with experience consciousness ages as well as the body. If man is what time and he himself together have made him, is it not against all nature to expect death in some mysterious way to put back the clock, to give him once again a freshness of perception which time has already withdrawn from him?

To such a school of thought, life itself offers sharp evidence against all notions of survival.

3

Others point out that even if survival in some way does come about, it does not necessarily follow that it will bring an improvement in our condition at all. Many ancient Greeks appeared to think it will not, and so also do some psychical researchers, who hold after scrutinising the modern evidence that, even if perhaps bodily death is in some way survived, it suggests no more than a process of continuing impoverishment, an inactive and taskless condition in which the psyche gradually fades and withers as its memories fade. The proud captain of his soul may find himself with less and less to command, and finally vanish completely, craft and all.

4

Countless other people, of course, entirely without reference to mediumistic evidence, believe firmly in survival. Many of these people would abhor any help from mediumship.

Nature's causality, regarded alone, may indeed seem to point sternly towards individual extinction. But to these people other factors within human nature itself, of a striking though more impalpable kind, suggest that we are not entirely identified with the body and its lessening powers, but indeed transcend it. If this is the true image of man, then he may truly be worth survival. Survival may be the very thing which distinguishes him from outer nature.

If there is a part of man which will survive death, then by logic this part must already be living within him now. Why should it be impossible, then, for that part to discover its own nature from within? "Man, know thyself." Self-knowledge may whisper an interior conviction of survival. Self-knowledge of course can be blinded by human fears or desires for certainty; it is possible to dismiss all belief in survival as the product of false religious teaching, or as some form of wish-fulfilment. But to a large number amongst the many millions who have reached a belief in it without the aid of external evidence, the idea of survival comes as an interior recognition of their own essential nature; they feel that they are already aware, even if dimly, of the existence within them of a partly hidden self in which lies their true future, present intimations of a surviving, even of an immortal part of themselves. In Wordsworthian phrase, "We feel that we are greater than we know."

5

Now what if there is involved another factor altogether? In his approach to the problem of survival, man usually places all the initiative upon himself; he takes it for granted that it is he who attempts the discovery, or alternatively satisfies himself that nothing exists to discover. But is this wholly true? How, after all, has the opportunity come about to get to know something of a possible life after death, something of the selves both of past friends and of guides who purport to communicate? They appear, not by our initiative but by their own. There is no way of summoning them up, as many mediums and would-be mediums have found.

Have the dead, then, themselves chosen this particular stage of world history, to prove their existence and their continued interest in the earth? The inauguration by the dead of a new chapter in human relationships is not an impossible conception.

Yet if such an attempt is being made, how sorry, how grotesque was its start! The first evidences of a purposive kind are usually said to have begun a hundred years ago with alleged knockings on the wall of a cottage at Hydesville by a pedlar who had been murdered there. The first mediums were accused of fraud, made signed confessions, and then repudiated them. Not an impressive nor a respectable beginning, nor was the further history of the early years at all edifying. Early mediumship was, much of it, of a crude kind, whether in the shape of materialisations or mental phenomena. Yet, as we know, by the 1880s, these happenings had been reported frequently enough to warrant the founding of the S.P.R. At about this time also the Rev. Stainton Moses's *Spirit Teachings* records one of the first attempts of a guide, by question and answer, to widen and break down the orthodox religious thought of that time, an attempt which his medium for long resisted. Then, between the wars, there appears to have begun a concerted effort from a number of guides to set up independent groups working in private, in which teaching of a more refined kind could be given than is possible in public churches, and asking for strenuous work by each individual upon his own character.

The facts, although they do not compel it, are at least in conformity with the notion that each phase in turn may have been initiated from those who claim to have survived death, and that each stage marks a step from the cruder to the more refined.

6

Now if men do survive and can give evidence of it, it would after all be very odd if communication were to confine itself only to proof and no more. For proof is a requirement imposed by living men, and a somewhat artificial requirement at that. Once the limitations imposed by the demands of evidence are surmounted, there could follow the forging of a new and changed relationship with old friends. Such a relationship in turn may be more pervasive than is expected or at first realised.

Another, a disturbing, factor now arises. If man does survive death, it is a pure assumption that it is impossible, other than through mediumship, for the surviving part of a man to have any further influence upon his fellows still living on earth. Such influences may arise not only by the occasional and third-party opportunities afforded by mediumship, but in a much closer way.

Mediumship may be an open illustration of what is really a much more continual though largely hidden process. The central purposes of mediumship may not lie in proof of survival at all. The production of evidence may just be an early effort, so to speak, by which survivors gain our attention. Mediumship may be an indicator of something much less specialised, something potentially common to all in the shape of quickened perception towards the living as well as the dead, faculties which are as yet too dim to function realiably in the majority of people.

The discarnate unanimously declare that the carrying out of both personal and impersonal tasks is and must always remain the responsibility of the living; they cannot take over our tasks. This does not preclude the possibility of receiving advice and some measure of collaboration, even if the dangers of mischievous discarnate interference and of nebulous ramblings from the unconscious stand in the way. What if criminal and saint alike can bring about at times a telepathic permeation of thought and emotion directly into the unconscious self of living men, whence it may well up later and influence them, for better or worse? Such a hypothetical invisible and silent assault upon the sanctity of the self is a profoundly repugnant idea to many, especially perhaps to those who admit sanctity in no other form.

Bizarre, disconcerting, or on the other hand profoundly reassuring as this idea may be, no enquirer into survival can neglect to ask what influence – if survival be true – can play, perhaps almost continually, upon the living from the dead.

Quite without respect for our opinions and beliefs, we may be surrounded by a crowd of unseen witnesses, with whose help or hindrance our best and worst ideas and impulses are sometimes born. We may have a smaller influence upon ourselves than we have supposed.

If we were able to raise the threshold of our consciousness in some way, should we then *all* find ourselves in touch with the dead? Some hold telepathy and mediumship to be the beginnings of a planned discarnate effort to bring a further horizon into western minds, at present somewhat over-rigidly bounded by strictly intellectual concepts and values. What if in some way the dead have been enabled to draw nearer than ever before to reassure us, and to work with us and help us to raise life to new standards, and, with their help, slowly change the face of mortal existence.

Mediumship with its uncertainties seems at first a most unlikely source from which any startling future advance can be expected. It can also seem nonsensical to suppose that mankind can develop qualities of consciousness which apparently set aside the general limits of human faculties which have been accepted as natural over thousands of years. But this would be a hasty conclusion; eastern religions from time immemorial have inculcated extended states of consciousness to which the mundane western world has largely remained unbelieving and indifferent. The superstitions of today sometimes become the facts of tomorrow, and vice versa.

Mediumship, then, in its very imperfect way, can point beyond itself to a possible future enlargement of consciousness, of a kind which may eventually prove acceptable to western life, and to a recognition of activities which are constantly playing upon human life, but of which we are not yet normally aware.

Whilst the inner faculties which are thus possibly possessed remain clouded, doubted, and denied, there is still need for demonstration after demonstration of mediumship. Whenever good quality mediumship is produced, there is always a greater demand for it than it can satisfy. Far better use needs to be made of the mediumship potential.

By always demanding quality in mediumship, by paying disciplined attention to its results, by providing the conditions which it needs in order to develop harmoniously, in fact by creating a serious instead of an idle audience for it, its true scope, and its limits too, must eventually be discovered.

In this way men and women of integrity can train themselves to assess it at every level of reality open to them, bringing their sharpest powers of experience to the careful and cautious putting of mediumistic material to the proof in normal life. A valuable pool of experience can be collected.

The production of intensified and purposive mediumship, its elucidation by objective scrutiny and subjective assessment, the recognition of difficulties which communicators struggle to overcome, the subjecting of the advice of guides to the hard school of practical experience – these tasks, unsatisfactory though they often seem in the performance, suggest a field which may lead far beyond the small corner of abnormal psychology to which science has so far banished mediumship. If its real place is a more honourable one than this, then to what other human faculties can it be related?

7

Here is a quotation from the Willett scripts:

> It was a radiant morning – haze on the mountains – ... but ... as I was leaving Nyon (by the steamer), I saw a great white mass – so high I took it at first to be a cloud. As we steamed towards Geneva it came more fully into view, and I suddenly realised it must be Mont Blanc – longed for but not seen by me since my arrival. Seen across the intense blue of the lake, and over a range of lower mountains, it was wonderfully beautiful.
>
> I sat down and gazed – then suddenly I heard the words "The Dark Young Man" – not with my ears but inside my mind – as if someone had said it to me in a world where thoughts pass without speech – I hadn't thought of the Dark Young Man for more than a year I am sure – and have been thinking and reading about nothing likely to revive the thought of him.
>
> Someone said, "He's helping you," and quite suddenly I seemed to tumble into a pool of knowledge – "Of course he's been helping you all the time."
>
> I got no sense of who was the speaker, but the Dark Young Man in the flash of a moment was there – quite close to me ... We stood there side by side looking at Mont Blanc and the lake and the colour of it all – but especially at the great tower of snow – All sorts of things kept passing through my mind too quickly to seize – a precious moment of human companionship. I don't know how long it lasted – it was like a day-dream yet more real than any reality of waking life.*

Many extra-sensory perceptions are not primarily concerned with the bringing of evidence, but have the character of an enriching inner experience. From the scientific viewpoint, nothing in Mrs. Willett's account can be verified. To her it was a process of sharing of something bestowed by another consciousness, and it clearly brought about in turn an intensification of her own. Two things in it are of interest, apart from the beauty of the experience which the medium's account conveys. One of these things is the inter-blending of the inner experience with the outward physical scene before her; the beauty of Mont Blanc co-existed and blended with the extra-sensory perception; neither cancelled the other out. The other thing is the fragility of the experience; her sense of the Dark Young Man could clearly be shattered and disappear in an instant; it was not easy to hold intact.

Mozart wrote an account of how he composed:

> Nor do I hear in my imagination the parts successively, but I hear them, as it were, all at once ... What a delight this is I cannot tell.†

* *Proc.*, Vol. 43, p. 81.

† Modern editors prefer to discount this letter as unauthentic, because there is no MS., and probably also on account of the unusual contents.

From the scientific aspect it makes complete nonsense. How can something so essentially expressed in time and succession as music be heard instantaneously, telescoped together? Of course, as with other paranormal experiences, one can choose to doubt that it ever took place. If it is accepted that it did, one thing is important to note; the experience took place when Mozart, as the same letter goes on to say, was "completely myself, entirely alone, and of good cheer". The extra-sensory perception took place at the very centre of his experience; there was nothing peripheral about it.

In a famous passage in mystical literature, St. Teresa of Avila describes an interior experience:

> I saw an angel close by me . . . in his hand a long spear of gold, and at the iron's point there seemed to be a little fire. He appeared to me to be thrusting it into my heart . . . he seemed . . . to leave me all on fire with a great love of God. The pain was so great that it made me moan; and yet so surpassing was the sweetness of this excessive pain that I could not wish to be rid of it. The soul is satisfied now with nothing less than God. The pain is not bodily, but spiritual; though the body has its share in it, even a large one. It is a caressing of love so sweet which now takes place between the soul and God, that I pray God of his goodness to make him experience it who may think I am lying.*

One may put this into a Freudian context; one may deny the existence of angels; but the positive content of the experience makes it, again, an extra-sensory perception, however unverifiable. Few besides the saints have reached to similar experiences, but the lesser experience of thousands who have pursued the mystical life in or out of convents leads to their giving weight to Teresa's account, and that surely is veridicality of a kind. After all Teresa herself is considered a touchstone of sanity and reason in this difficult interior world of religious experience.

Hagiolatry apart, the lives of saints appear to abound in mediumistic experiences of varied sorts, and of very varying value. Teresa herself received "The Interior Castle" by a process akin to that of automatic writing. But there is one big difference; the automatist usually functions at a level below that of her writings, is more truly an amanuensis, but Teresa's extra-sensory faculties when they arose were, so to speak, fully possessed by her, in that for the time being she could live consciously and with the whole of herself at that level. The merely reflect-

* *Autobiography*, ch. 29, Sections 16–17.

ing, "borrowed" element in much mediumship, as seen in the episode of the Dark Young Man, is far below the experience of the saint. Yet these belong together, and Mozart's experience as well, somewhere in a common realm of extra-sensory perception.

8

What all have in common – mystic, artist, medium – is an enhanced state of consciousness which by its very nature cannot be continuously held, cannot be sustained through the whole of everyday living. The artist has to express his inescapable sense of perfection in a form of beauty belonging to this world; his primary concern is with the vessel in which the sacred liquid is held. The mystic moves into, and temporarily shares, a realm of being utterly beyond the grasp of the normal mind, a realm which is almost incommunicable, and by the light of which all the values of this world seem as nothing.

The much more humble task of the medium is to become aware of something of the knowledge and of the consciousness which discarnate minds possess, at whatever varied levels these exist.

When the medium succeeds in truly raising her consciousness she seems able to step, for however brief a space, into an area of intensified meaning and order which lies within some at least of the discarnate minds influencing her, and which the latter say also reflects the nature and character of the realm in which they live. When she steps up to his level of consciousness instead of the communicator stepping down to hers, his meaning reaches the medium with a sense of inner coherence which she cannot resist or challenge. This intensification, and the deepening it brings, is what the best mediums are aiming for. Here her normal consciousness, that which she possesses whilst not operating as a medium, is of some significance. Like the artist's, the personality of the medium becomes intensified as she works, yet in neither can the daily personality be dismissed as a mere surplusage, a sediment little related to the valuable essence. The basic gift, the talent, it is true, seems to bear some curious irrelevance to the essential nature of the personality. The artist's vision may be trivial, the undisciplined medium may be a vain sparrow-brain. But the larger the essential moral nature informing either, and the more varied and complete the skills and attributes which are available, the greater the product of the basic talent is likely to be.

That a medium can communicate with the next world is no more in itself than a basic talent like the artist's ability to draw, and the medium who reports nothing but trivial thoughts and preoccupations, who describes her communicators' faces without ever penetrating into their minds, who is attuned only to vulgar and selfish emotions, cannot organise her gift to the general profit any more than can the seaside artist who is content to draw over and over again the same thatched cottage and crudely coloured flower-garden.

The medium, like the artist and mystic, cannot fully sustain her vision when she turns to interpreting it. When she touches a level of consciousness deeper than her own, and then attempts to pass on to her sitter what she has thus glimpsed, inevitably, as she breaks it down into words, it suffers a diminution. The vision exceeds her expression of it.

In trance, too, when the discarnate consciousness makes its own choice of expression from the meagre resources it finds available for its use within the medium's mind, an equivalent diminution must be expected.

The deepest activities which mediumship has yet reached must be looked upon as a form of very imperfect partnership; the best it can offer is an interpretation, a translation, from which, whether in trance or otherwise, a measure of subjective colouration is never absent. Like a literary translation, it has to be looked upon as falling below the level of significance of the original. Hence the discarnate Myers's frequent exasperation with his mediums. Hence the constant discipline of the true medium in her daily life to train her receptive faculties to be as free from agitation and distortion as possible.

In this process of translation or interpretation, the listener or pupil has an important even a decisive part. For the medium, again like the artist, does not speak primarily to herself, her task is to communicate. Upon the listener's response depends, to a great extent, the depth of teaching which can gradually be given; if he fails to respond, or only responds very slowly, the pace of the teacher is halted too. In trance teachings an element of repetition is found, which though it must be partly due to comparative insensitivities in the mind of even the most sensitive medium, is undoubtedly also largely due to slowness in the pupil's own response. If he fails to put what is taught into practice in his daily life, of what use is it for the teacher to pass on to further lessons?

We would explain that we can only give a little knowledge. Through all the years that our (Lodge) has been working, the . . . brethren have only released a very little wisdom at a time. The aim is to bring aspirants for the truth along the path gently, and very slowly. In our talks we shall repeat ourselves from time to time . . .

We know that you are by nature inquisitive; that you want to rush into the temple and you want to . . . know more and more about these ancient mysteries. Well, you can know more, my brethren; you can know more if you will only provide the necessary conditions for the unfoldment of your understanding. You will never gain the knowledge that you crave for simply by reading books; you will only gain the knowledge for which you long, you will only reach the end of your search, through living, through daily experience, through contact with your fellow men.*

The teacher can but repeat and repeat in different ways until the meaning is assimilated, until the pupil has proved willing to come to know himself better, to suffer, and in doing so to find the way to new levels of experience.

9

Some ancient civilisations, those of Egypt, China and the classical world, have already claimed communications rather like those we are now exploring – and so do some primitive twentieth-century tribes. Leaving aside the interior visions and counsellings which abound in the religious life and which often appear to derive from elevated states of consciousness, it needs to be faced that history – or what history knows about communications – prefers the view that over these thousands of years exterior communications have more often than not brought about illusions and uncertainties; have not the great world religions always been right in fighting shy of mediumship?

To this severe question, it has to be answered that surely modern man needs desperately any genuine extension of his knowledge of life, and if these communicators establish even their own existence, this in itself is a momentous first step, from which much may subsequently lead. Such communication can readily be abused and most probably was in the past. Will man now learn to make a better use of it, a disinterested use, which will not bring illusion upon himself, as a result of debasing it by exploiting it for his own selfish ends?

The present deliberate advance upon us made by survivors, if such it is, can be no historical accident, but foreseen as possible and appropriate in an age in which gigantic political and commercial powers

* *Student Teaching* (White Eagle), Nos. 231 and 243.

threaten to deprive man of many of his human values, and much of his individuality – something even more important than its threats through atomic warfare to life itself.

Mere evidence for survival cannot take us far. By itself it can be no substitute for the essential contributions of the great religions, when stripped of dogmatic encrustations, to the enrichment of the interior nature of man. Yet to become convinced that a dead friend or lover still lives and speaks to one can be a shatteringly direct and vivid experience. But a demonstration of survival, in the phrase of the posthumous Myers, is only the presenting of credentials.

Yet it is usually by first bringing to us conviction of the survival of our imperfect earth friends, and thus, by inference, conviction of one's own survival, that other wiser beings gradually bring us in time to accept their own reality. In turn, the *value* of the survival of our own relatives, however vivid it may seem at first, stands or falls in the last resort by the wisdom or otherwise of these guides. For if among the dead no wiser beings can ever be found, living at a deeper level of purpose than we ourselves know as yet, there is little point to be seen in surviving at all; our own communicators may appear to be very animated, but if they never grow and change, then, for all we can tell, they are really little more than helpless, passive shades. But if wiser beings do appear, and if we can recognise them to be such, then we recognise that we too are worth survival; for in them we see foreshadowed our own eventual future.

10

People of intellectual ability, before turning to the difficult evidential fields of survival, assume that what brains of good calibre have discovered will be found within the records of psychical research, and that the fantasies which wishful emotions and muddled thinking have built up over the years will be found in Spiritualism.

However, when the intellectual begins a serious first-hand investigation – whether drawn to it by intellectual interest or driven to it by some unsatisfied personal need – the picture changes as soon as he leaves the paper records behind him. He enters a third field which is neither that of scientific records nor a fantasy escape-world; he is called on to assess evidence relating to his own life and being, instead of that of a third party.

He comes ready to use his critical faculties in an impersonal and disinterested way which will leave him quite untouched. What he finds, provided he makes successful contact with his mediums, is another mind which concentrates its own insight on him. The initiative is reversed; instead of his examining the subject on his own terms, he finds that he also is being examined. He probably has not expected this reversal.

When the subject thus comes to life as it were from outside him and moves in upon him, refusing to remain a static object on the far side of his intellectual defences, the decisive part of the enquiry begins. He is first likely to ask himself whether this apparent intelligence arises from some temporary amalgam of the medium's perceptions with his own. Subsequently he may come to feel obliged to associate part of this intelligence with some person long known to him who is now dead; later still he may associate another part of it with a hypothetical being, whom he cannot get to know except with the medium's help, but who seems to possess at times this surprising and disconcerting insight into him. He finds that this intelligence has continuity, and appears again as it did a month or a year before, taking up the threads as if there had been no interruption. This intelligence is also found to possess depth, for it has access to insight not necessarily shared by the enquirer. In fact it behaves like a mature and independent being.

Now if all this seems to happen, the enquirer gradually has to involve one facet of his being after another to deal with what is introduced. Judgment is ineffective until he has tried out in action at least some of the insights offered to him about himself. So he himself becomes the subject and centre of the experiment. Until he embarks thus far – and of course there need be no hurry about it – he is not really committed in any worthwhile way to this third field. Indeed many prefer always to remain safely in retreat within the arid walls of intellectual comment.

Any real committal in this field, long before any final judgment is taken, usually finds itself accompanied by a rising sense of hope. If life does continue after death then certainly the worst fear which plagues humanity is removed, but logic says also that if many of a man's remaining ills are going to continue because they are part of the flaws, poverties and excesses of his own inner nature, then he may be worse off after death, since these ills could remain with him for a far longer period than on earth. But the hope which wells up from a deep, unknown spring within, does not judge it so. Discarnate communicators do more than make assertions about survival and about some of the laws of existence; they quietly demonstrate them. If the investigator comes to accept these demonstrations, his hope gradually develops into a growing inner certainty that the laws of cause and effect truly in operation are not those of a "heartless, witless nature", but are ultimately profoundly moral in causation. In a limited way, they can be seen by him at work within and upon himself, and in particular they show how his own inner flaws can be overcome. Without orthodox religious dogmas, and certainly without the shallow confidence with which Spiritualists suppose that death in next to no time will largely end all their troubles, he finds that he comes to share more and more the viewpoint of his communicators, that the world, behind all its problems and horrors, is one in which one's whole nature can and does finally and utterly acquiesce. To the intellectual this is often seen as nothing but a stupid assumption which passes altogether beyond the facts of life. But this hope, and the certainty which communicators own and impart, are clues which once received can become hard to ignore. Their certainty rides serenely above the logic of the intellect; man cannot help but find it so; he can accept such a certainty or deny it, but he cannot alter its nature. The experiences which communicators impart convince him not only from without, but from within himself as well, that man does survive; that it is necessary for him to do so, since communicators, apart from demonstrating their survival as a fact, show that they find themselves governed by a sense and purpose in the universe which requires of man that he shall survive.

Rational and orderly collection and assessment of evidence, necessary and admirable though they are, cannot bring about a true sense of survival. They can of course bring about a conviction of it. But mental proof alone always has a missing part – that response which a man's nature can make from within.

The constant hesitations, so justified and reasonable, of many researchers to commit themselves are not readily overcome. The rationalist can dismiss acceptance of survival as *always* being no more than a delusion of the feelings. Between the man who has come to accept survival and the rationalist who has not, it has to be admitted that a gulf exists.

There is a class of facts which everyone can accept as indisputable; nobody doubts, for instance, that fire burns. Survival is in no way a fact of this kind, however strong the demonstration of it may become.

This is because the facts require a response; they do not guarantee themselves, though many would like to make them do so, thereby casting off personal responsibility for the individual discovery of them which is necessary. The fact of survival, masked by the present seeming contradictions of evidence, can only fully be known when a man is willing to step forth for himself and use his own responses and insights, as working tools needed to discover it.

Therefore a scientific hypothesis of survival, however strong, can at best stamp only one side of the coin; a man's own powers of dealing with his own evidence and experience, his interior endorsements of it, and his resulting discoveries of or about his self which will survive, are needed to stamp the coin's other side.

The efforts, the mistakes, and the limitations of communication; its frustrations and seeming blank contradictions; the reassurance it sometimes brings; the consolation, and the shafts of insight into self; the exclusiveness forced upon the psychical researcher by his methods and the lack of vision of many survivalists; the voices which bring consolation and spiritual teaching, or sometimes the babbling of empty words; the utter inward certainty of survival which can enter as of itself into the heart; all these compete and conflict with one another in the individual's search for truth and for his own truth.

The purpose of a guide is to work upon his pupil so as to set into operation a process of inner knowing. The production of evidence begins to nudge it on its way. The guide then nourishes a man's hidden inner resources, and demonstrates their existence in him, until this brings about a gradual conviction of the indestructibility of that part of him which can only be known in this inner way. This process of conviction is impalpable, subtle and hard to describe, yet unmistakable to anyone in whom it comes to pass; it is of course something which the religions of the world in various forms and manners of their own have already discovered and rediscovered countless times.

II

That one's personality will survive, lock stock and barrel, as an immortal, is certainly a very queer notion. Spiritualism with vulgar ease would often grant the gift of immortality to thoughts and feelings which can readily be recognised as little more worthy of it than is the physical body.

If man's stumbling imperfect self does survive, then what is before him must surely be expected to include a process of discarding as well as one of gaining. Those who consider the earthly personality too worthless to survive death will then, to a measure, be correct, even if this point of view overlooks another side of man which *is* worthy of survival. Survival may prove to be a long-term opportunity to *qualify* for immortality, to discover and foster whatever known or unknown qualities in a man can deserve immortality; surely a man must do much more than merely die in order to qualify for that. Qualifying may be a very long-term process indeed. It may already have had its commencement on earth. The rare and precious individualities of some of the saints may demonstrate the beginnings of such an achievement in their earth lives. To talk, from beyond the grave, of immortality means little as testimony unless something of the shape of what it involves can be seen too to be demonstrated in their own selves by wise and possibly ancient beings as they counsel living men. Then the latter may in turn begin to understand it, and go on to develop some small part of it in themselves during their life on earth.

Each may discover a fragment of his immortal self, as much of it as he can bear to know, and begin to live out that self here and now. Once immortality enters into the picture as a process of *becoming*, which operates in men whilst they are still on earth, life then completely changes its perspective and ceases to be a race against death.

What are the implications of such intimations? The very experience of living, to the degree to which it is accepted, becomes a demonstration – or, as some would regard it, a puzzle to be unravelled in infinitely varied ways – which slowly and surely reveals what is worthy and worthless in man himself.

To survive means that there can be no escape, either from fellow men whom we have wronged, or from ourselves whom thereby we have wronged the more. The results of betrayals can indeed be left behind on earth, but the men betrayed are met again. More important, the necessity to put these betrayals right arises and lives on inexorably in a man's own heart. Errors, conflicts and injustices have to be resolved by the creators of them. "There is nothing covered, that shall not be revealed; and hid, that shall not be known."

This necessity is a far larger thing than the saving of one's moral skin; there is no system of rewards and punishments, but only impersonal consequences. Desire for personal prestige and the quest for salvation become blots upon one's escutcheon; indeed the escutcheon itself vanishes as something meaningless. The competition of life shows itself to be an illusion; a different and grander purpose replaces self-hood. There can be no leaving behind of laggards; no passing by on the other side of the road, for there is no individual goal, but only a common goal: the participation by all in the attributes of immortality, which cannot be fully enjoyed until all men, helping and being helped, have reached them.

The concept of time becomes indefinitely enlarged. The point of a life is no longer how much can be fitted into it, but the quality of what is done. In this enormously larger framework, effort becomes a peaceful thing, since there is the whole of time ahead for fulfilment, instead of just one lifetime. With knowledge of a personal guide comes realisation of a degree of loving co-operation to be drawn upon. The wearisome burden of the personal self can be gradually cast off, the qualities of immortality gradually learned and taken on. There is no room for death.

12

In posthumous words claiming to be those of Professor Sidgwick, founder and first President of the S.P.R.

> ... We no more solve the riddle of Death by dying than we solve the problem of Life by being born – Take my own case – I was always a seeker – until it seemed at times as if the quest was more to me than the prize – Only the attainments of my search were generally like rainbow gold always beyond and afar – It is not all clear – I seek still – only with a confirmed optimism more perfect and beautiful than any we imagined before ... The Solution of the Great Problem I could not give you – I am still very far away from it and the abiding knowledge of the inherent truth and Beauty into which all the inevitable uglinesses of Existence finally resolve themselves will be yours in due time.*

> * *Proc.*, Vol. 21, p. 319.

BOOKS FOR FURTHER READING

Psychical Research

Proceedings of Society for Psychical Research
Proceedings of American Society for Psychical Research
Proceedings of Boston Society for Psychical Research
Human Personality and its survival of bodily death. F. W. H. Myers
Thirty Years of Psychical Research. Prof. Charles Richet (from the French)
Supernormal Faculties in Man. E. Osty (from the French)
From the Conscious to the Unconscious. G. Geley (from the French)
Discarnate Influence in Human Life. Prof. E. Bozzano (from the Italian)
The Survival of Man. Oliver Lodge
Evidence of Personal Survival from Cross-Correspondences. H. F. Saltmarsh
Evidence of Identity. Kenneth Richmond
Evidence of Purpose. Zoe Richmond
Experimental Psychical Research. Dr. R. H. Thouless
New Frontiers of the Mind. Prof. J. B. Rhine
The Personality of Man. G. N. M. Tyrrell
Zoar. W. H. Salter
The Enigma of Survival. Prof. Hornell Hart

General

The Imprisoned Splendour. Prof. Raynor C. Johnson
Watcher on the Hills. Prof. Raynor C. Johnson
The Light and the Gate. Prof. Raynor C. Johnson
The Sixth Sense. Rosalind Heywood
Man's Latent Powers. Phoebe Payne
The Psychic Sense. Phoebe Payne and Dr. L. J. Bendit
Knowledge of the Higher Worlds. Rudolf Steiner

Evidence chiefly through one Sensitive
Life Beyond Death with Evidence. Rev. C. Drayton Thomas
Some New Evidence for Human Survival. Rev. C. Drayton Thomas
The Bridge. Nea Walker
The Psychic Bridge. Jane Sherwood
Personality Survives Death. Lady Barrett
Swan on a Black Sea. Geraldine Cummins

Autobiographical
My Life as a Search for the Meaning of Mediumship. Eileen J. Garrett
My Life in Two Worlds. Gladys Osborne Leonard
The Infinite Hive. Rosalind Heywood

Books based on Scripts or Trance Communications
The Road to Immortality. Geraldine Cummins
Beyond Human Personality. Geraldine Cummins
The Return of Arthur Conan Doyle. Ivan Cooke
Spiritual Unfoldment. ("White Eagle")
A "Silver Birch" Anthology.
Spirit Teachings. Rev. Stainton Moses
More Spirit Teachings. Rev. Stainton Moses

Index

Index

A
Aeschylus, 58
Astor, 136

B
Balfour, Lord Arthur, 60, 150
   Francis, 150
   (*See also* "Dark Young Man")
   Gerald, 67, 69, 94, 105, 150, 152
Barrett, Sir W., 97, 122, 126
Bayfield, Rev. M. A., 68, 138, 146
Beauchamp, Sally, 32, 137
Bergson, Prof., 31, 148
Birge-Pratt, 66
Bourne, Canon, 19
Bozzano, Prof. E., 35
Brittain, Annie, 79, 81
Browne, H. J., 27

C
Cervantes, 120
Clairvoyance, 16
College of Psychic Science, 56
Conley, Michael, 22-3
Conrad, Joseph, 14
Cooper, Mrs., 36
Crookes, Sir W., 122, 125, 126
Cross-correspondence, 58, 59-61
Cummins, G., 62, 98, 132, 136, 137, 149, 150

D
"Dark Young Man", 104, 150, 159, 160

Darwin, 121
Davis, Gordon, 35, 36
Dawson-Smith, 79-84
Direct voice, 8
Dodds, Prof. E. R., 46
Dodson, Miss, 21-2
Doyle, A. C., 141, 142
Drayton Thomas, Rev. C. D., 93, 133
   Etta, 93, 94, 114, 115
   Rev. John, 90, 93, 97, 114, 126, 133
Ducasse, C. J., 37 (note)

E
Ear of Dionysius, 61
Eckener, 124
"Eve", 32, 137

F
Feda, 80, 90, 92-6, 112-15, 126, 135-7
"Ferguson", 36, 45
Finney, Julia, 53-4

G
Garrett, Eileen, 123, 124
Gill, Jordan, 56
Goddard, Sir V., 125
Gurney, Edmund, 21, 62, 94, 105, 106, 108

H
Hallucinations, Census of, 18

Hinchliffe, Capt., 124
　Mrs., 124
Hobbes, 21
Hodgson, Dr. R., 25, 30, 44, 53, 54
Holland, Mrs., 91
Homer, 103
Horace Ode, 58
Hyperacuity, 13, 15
Hypnosis, 31
Hyslop, Dr. J., 30

I
Irwin, Flt. Lt. H. C., 123

J
Johnson, Prof. Raynor, 136, 147
Johnston, 124
Jung, 32

K
Kipling, Mrs., 14
Knight, Wilson, 51

L
Latin message, 58
Leonard, Mrs., 62, 79, 80, 92, 112–14, 122, 145
Leonie, 32
Levitation, 7
Lodge, Sir Oliver, 30, 31, 53, 55, 56, 62, 65, 66, 69, 83, 105, 108, 139, 152
　Raymond, 65–6
London Spiritualist Alliance, 56
Lord's Prayer, 58
Lyttelton, Hon. Mary, 60

M
Mace, Prof. C. A., 39
Maloy, 38–9
Mare, W. de la, 149
Materialisation, 7
Menneer, 21

M'Kay, 38
M.N. case, 113
Moses, Rev. Stainton, 45, 156
Mozart, 159, 160
Murray, Dr. G., 14, 15, 146, 147, 148
　Lord, 14
Myers, F. W. H., 54–63, 89–91, 98–101, 106–8, 125–7, 132, 133, 137, 162

N
Newbolt, Celia, 14

O
Ossowiecki, 16
Ovid, 58
Oxyrhynchus papyrus, 117

P
Palm Sunday, 60, 150
Pearce, 41
Pearl Tie-pin, 27, 53
Pelham, George, 24–6, 29, 31, 34, 44–6, 53, 59
Personality, secondary and multiple, 32–4, 135–7
Phinuit, 113, 126, 137, 138
Piddington, 63
Piper, Mrs., 25, 30, 31, 34, 44, 45, 58, 59, 113, 137
Plotinus, 58
Poltergeist, 7
Posthumous message, 53–6
Pratt, Ambrose, 98, 136
Proceedings of S.P.R., 3, 5, 13, 29, 49

Q
Q., Lady, 16

R
Ramsden-Miles, 15, 34
Red Cloud, 117
Rhine, Prof. J. B., 40, 41

Richet, Prof. C., 42, 65
Rosher, Grace, 125
R.101, 53, 122-5

S

Scott, Capt., 123
Shark, 27, 53
Sidgwick, Nora, 69, 70, 139, 149
　Prof. H., 69, 108, 169
Slate-writing, 7
Soal, Dr. S. G., 35, 36, 41, 45
Spiritualism, 140-4
S.P.R., 3, 4, 43, 50, 51, 55, 59, 131, 148, 149, 156, 169
Statius, 61, 68, 138, 146
Strindberg, 14

T

Telepathy, 13-23
　Extended, 34-40
　Super, *see* Telepathy Extended
Teresa, St., of Avila, 160

Thaw, Dr., 137
Thouless, Dr. R. H., 56-7
Tolstoy, 148
Toynbee, Mrs. A., 14
Trotwood, Betsy, 53
Tyrrell, G. N. M., 69

V

Verrall, Dr. A. W., 68, 69, 138
　Mrs., 55, 59, 60, 61, 62
Villiers, Major O., 123

W

Wax casts, 7
Wellington, 21
White Eagle, 117
Willett, Mrs., 62, 67, 90, 94, 101, 104, 106-9, 149, 150-2, 159
Wilmot, 19-20

Z

Zener cards, 40-3, 147